# TYRIAN INFLUENCE IN THE UPPER GALILEE

MEIRON EXCAVATION PROJECT

edited by

Eric M. Meyers

Meiron Excavation Project, vol. 1: *Ancient Synagogue Excavations at Khirbet Shema$^c$*, *Upper Galilee, Israel 1970-1972*, by Eric M. Meyers, A. Thomas Kraabel, James F. Strange. Annual of the American Schools of Oriental Research 42. Durham, NC: Duke University Press, 1976.

Number 2

TYRIAN INFLUENCE IN THE UPPER GALILEE

by

Richard S. Hanson

# TYRIAN INFLUENCE IN THE UPPER GALILEE

by

Richard S. Hanson

Published by

American Schools of Oriental Research

Distributed by

American Schools of Oriental Research
126 Inman St.
Cambridge, MA 02139

# TYRIAN INFLUENCE IN THE UPPER GALILEE

by

Richard S. Hanson

Cover design by Suellen Feinberg

Library of Congress Cataloging in Publication Data

Hanson, Richard S.
  Tyrian influence in the Upper Galilee.

  (Meiron excavation project; v. 2)
  Bibliography: p.
  1. Tyre—History.  2. HaGalīl Ha Elyon,
Israel—Antiquities.  3. Tyre—Commerce
—Israel—HaGalīl Ha Elyon.  4. HaGalīl
Ha Elyon, Israel—Commerce—Lebanon—
Tyre.  5. Numismatics, Phoenician.  6. Nu-
mismatics—Israel—HaGalīl   Ha   Elyon.
I. American Schools of Oriental Research.
II. Title.  III. Series.
DS89.T8H36      939′.44      79-11775
ISBN 0-89757-504-0

Printed in the United States of America

# CONTENTS

# INTRODUCTION

With the publication of this short monograph, *Tyrian Influence in Upper Galilee*, the Meiron Excavation Project enters a new and significant stage of research. Beginning in 1970 with the excavation of Khirbet Shemaᶜ, continuing at ancient Meiron in 1971 until 1977, and commencing excavation at nearby Gush Ḥalav in 1977, the excavation team has endeavored from the outset to pursue the study of Galilee in its broadest, East Mediterranean setting as well as part of its larger regional context in Syria-Palestine.

R. S. Hanson has been a senior member of this staff from the beginning. Originally called upon to assist with both the anticipated epigraphic finds as well as numismatics, it soon became clear that our most important epigraphic materials were to be limited to those of the coins themselves. So rich has been the supply of coins, and so high has been the percentage of recoverability in cleaning that the shift in attention to numismatic concerns has been especially fortuitous. The high alkalinity of the Galilean soil has helped greatly to preserve in good condition the more than 4,000 coins that the author has identified to date.

One of the major achievements of the excavation team, and especially of Hanson's enormous energy, diligence, and industry, has been the practice of cleaning and provisionally identifying coins on site. The chronological value of the data provided by this convention has been inestimable and has allowed the excavators to refine greatly the ceramic typology of the Galilee in the Roman and Byzantine periods. After field readings of coins were made, a thorough reworking of these provisional identifications was done by the author back in the United States. Still another check on the material was made when the final report became available. The service rendered to the entire staff, therefore, has been extraordinary. More than any other feature of the methodology employed by the excavation team, this simple factor has made possible many unanticipated aspects of research. Chief among these results is this report on the city coins of Tyre unearthed in the Meiron Project excavations. Because of the close collaboration between excavator and numismatist, it became evident quite early that the high percentage of city coins found at each excavated site was most unusual. The reader of excavation reports might have expected a simple catalog of coin finds rather than the carefully selected mints presented here. He might also have expected such a publication later in a series. The present study, however, is presented as number two of a much larger series and represents an array of material excavated in the course of seven seasons of excavations at three sites. It represents a departure from usual publication schemes for several reasons.

First, since the excavation publishes a numismatic report and an index of coins by locus, together with the field reports, a seriatim listing or complete catalog is not the most pressing concern for our research team. Hopefully, at some future date, all of the data will be synthesized and cataloged in a way useful to both numismatists and archeologists, in another volume.

Second, because such a high incidence of excavated coins comes from Tyre itself, there is an inherent logic in presenting to the scholarly world a datum which has become one of the most basic assumptions and building blocks governing our work: that from the Hellenistic period until the end of the Roman period, the Upper Galilee was oriented toward the Phoenician coast at Tyre, at least economically.

This may not come as a surprise to some specialists, but for those who deal with Palestine in late antiquity it is a stunning piece of evidence which has great ramifications for both the historian of the period and for all scholars who labor to understand this supposedly remote corner in ancient Palestine. Therefore, the orientation of Upper Galilee to Tyre should be of paramount importance to the biblical scholar, the talmudist, and classicist alike. One of the common assumptions in the field of New Testament and Rabbinics, and also in the field of Palestinian archeology itself, has been that Galilee is a kind of backwater area from the point of view of topography and material culture. New Testament scholars in particular are apt to describe this remote region as the locale of the ꜥam haꜢaretz, "the people of the land," who are ignorant, poor of speech, and out of mainstream Judaism. A logical inference, often made, is that Galilee, especially in the far north, is a remote outpost set away from the dominant trends of the day.

Some of this may well be true. However, the present study, when taken into account with other materials uncovered during the course of excavation by the Meiron team, especially the ceramic evidence, will serve to bring about greater caution in evaluating the effects of topographic isolation. This study clearly indicates that the Meiron area, for all its isolation, is still trading and dealing with the great coastal city of Tyre. One must ask why the inhabitants of this region chose to trade in Tyre when the great coastal city of Akko-Ptolemais lay only slightly south and to the west along a convenient wadi valley that doubtlessly functioned as a well-traveled service road in antiquity. Or more to the point, why didn't the inhabitants of the Meiron area trade more with their brethren, during the rabbinic period at least, in the well-known city of Tiberias on the western shore of the Sea of Galilee, less than half the distance to Tyre, traveling down the Wadi Chorazin? Tiberias or neighboring Tarichaeae and other sites along the Kinneret stand astride the great Roman roads of the day and had access to the kinds of goods and services that might be required in Upper Galilee. So the decision of the villagers at Teqoꜥa, Meiron, and Gush Halav to trade on the Phoenician coast seems to be quite conscious. While all the reasons for this are not clear, several explanations are compelling. First, from the point of view of topography, Upper Galilee is truly oriented north toward Syria and the Phoenician coast. Second, and perhaps more to the point, the businessmen of this area received a better price in Tyre for their choice commodities.

The quotation from Josephus (J. W. 2.591-94) at the beginning of this work concerning the episode about John of Giscala is supportive of the latter solution. Explicit in the Josephan narrative is the assumption that Upper Galilee is particularly rich in olives and in the production of olive oil. Indeed, the olive oil of the Meiron region is the most famous of any area in rabbinic.

literature. The three sites which have been excavated by the Expedition are particularly singled out among all places in Galilee for the fame and purity of the olive oil. Even in early medieval times the quality of olive-oil production in the Meiron area was so legendary that it was assumed to have been used exclusively in the Temple in Jerusalem. So when John of Giscala invests in olive oil to amass a fortune, he is not only taking advantage of the local product but shrewdly taking into account the worth of his product where it is plentiful, Giscala, and where it is in demand, Tyre. The *J.W.* narrative clearly mentions that he buys in Tyrian currency, making a profit of 8:1. In the parallel account in *Life* (74) he makes an even larger profit of 10:1. Since at least one rabbinic source forbids the use of foreign oil (*b. ᶜAbod. Zar.* 36 a,b) lest it be tainted by unclean vessels, John is perhaps appealing to Jewish loyalties in Syria to purchase the pure Holy Land oil. The reluctance of Diasporan Jews to use pagan olive oil dates back to the reign of Seleucus I (*Ant.* 12.120). His motives, therefore, are quite transparent: sheer profiteering of the basest kind.

The point of all this is that while Jews might have traded predominantly with the city of Tyre—if we may take the large number of Tyrian mints found in our three Upper Galilean sites to indicate such a situation—this does not necessarily reflect a compromise of any sort of religious standards. On the contrary, we have seen how John of Giscala may have taken advantage even of Jewish law in order to amass a personal fortune, thereby violating only the ethics of fair play. On the other hand, it would be fatuous of us to assume that such trade and commerce did not bring the world of Upper Galilee into some direct, albeit limited, contacts with the cosmopolitan and pagan culture of that coastal center, some of which ultimately filtered back to the local villages. While such cultural contacts may not be visible at first, they perhaps enable us to explain some of the anomalies in Upper Galilee in the Roman period.

Ceramic forms, for example, point to a cultural affinity to the north and to western Gaulinitis, but the presence of many fine wares suggests that even these areas, which are relatively cut off from the southern and more Hellenized areas, also had joined the mainstream of material culture by the Late Roman period. Some scholars would place the origin of synagogue-building in the Syrian world in the Early Roman period, a possibility which becomes tenable when we are open to the notion that Upper Galilee, the center of most of the known examples of synagogue architecture, was less encapsulated and isolated from the important cultural and commercial centers of the day.

The late Michael Avi-Yonah explained the isolation of the Upper Galilee in the following manner. As the Romans set about to administer the province of Palestine after the two wars of 70 C.E. and 135 C.E., they began to implement their policies through a basic administrative reorganization. This entailed the establishment of cities as part of a general policy of urbanization. And yet of all the areas under Roman control, only Upper Galilee, referred to as Tetracomia, or "Four Villages" in Josephus, and the Golan remained outside of city districts. While Judea and Samaria were absorbed into a series of pagan city-states, Upper Galilee and the Golan were truly decentralized. Therefore, the question arises as to the motivation of Rome in sparing this region from her tightening controls. It might well be that Rome, recognizing that this area had become the new stronghold of those fleeing north, did not want to antagonize further the inhabitants of the Upper Galilee. After all, John of Giscala was perhaps better known for his rebel activities than for his commercial dealings. Not only did he successfully challenge Josephus' command of Upper Galilee, but he became one of the Zealotic leaders of the First Revolt in Jerusalem as well.

If there was a genuine desire on the part of the new population which was moving from the south to the north after the Roman wars to keep a good distance between them and Rome, then the choice of the Galilean highlands as a new center for their religion and culture was most appropriate. For in these hills there was already a coterie of people who had distinguished themselves as individuals somewhat removed from the dominant trends of the day. Perhaps that is why the New Testament remembers them in such a negative way. But still, it reflects very much upon the wisdom of the Roman government that the Upper Galilee was exempted from the usual policy of urbanization. The loose and decentralized Roman administration of this area, therefore, not only enabled peace to prevail after the Bar Kochba war but also enabled Jewish culture to survive and prosper.

In addition, it facilitated greatly the opportunity for the local population to trade in nearby Tyre. While historical data show the historic ties between Tyre and Israel, the numismatic data indicate an increase by around 13% in the supply of Tyrian coins in the Meiron area after the destruction of the Second Temple in 70 c.e. More than anything, this fact testifies to the quickening pace of existing commercial ties betweeen Tyre and the local inhabitants in this period. Not only did the Roman policy of decentralization foster indigenous culture in the religious sphere, but it served as a stimulus to the local economy as well.

Hanson's conclusion that Tyre was "the center of economic influence for a peripheral area that included Upper Galilee in its orbit" is thus one that has far-reaching importance for all further researches in northern Palestinian studies. In historical work one can often forget that modern political boundaries played no role in antiquity. But it now seems possible to consider the northern limits of Upper Galilee well into modern Lebanon, extending into the foothills of the Lebanon range itself. Avi-Yonah had wanted to place the northwestern limits of Upper Galilee at Marun er-Ras, which he had previously identified with the Meiron of our excavations. While still alive, however, he came to accept our identification of Meiron with the Meroth of Josephus. Only further research, especially survey work in southern Lebanon, will help define the northern limits of Galilee in the general area of Meiron.

Hanson's work, therefore, inaugurates a new phase of regional studies in Syro-Palestinian archeology. This work is also to be welcomed as a convenient introduction to the history of the city of Tyre, especially as viewed through numismatic data. The diverse cultural traditions which characterize the history of that city can be followed in his presentation of the iconographic materials preserved in their coinage. Furthermore, his brief history underscores the close commercial ties that existed between biblical Israel and that great Phoenician center. It is a revealing feature of ancient Near Eastern history that links established more than a millennium earlier in the reign of King Solomon continue to exert a heavy influence on major portions of postbiblical Israel, the heart and very core of which was in northern Galilee.

Eric M. Meyers
Duke University
Durham, N.C.
12 January 1978

# ACKNOWLEDGMENTS

Acknowledgments of gratitude, as usual, must go to several persons. First and foremost, I must acknowledge the leadership, organizational abilities, and the extraordinarily energetic efforts of Eric and Carol Meyers, who have become like a brother and sister to me in the midst of our mutual labors. To my gifted colleague, James F. Strange of the University of Southern Florida, I must express admiration as well as gratitude for his skillful and multitalented contributions. For bearing most of the costs of this publication I must thank the Meiron Expedition and Duke University. For help without which I could have accomplished nothing of this sort, I must thank my kindly friend, Hank van Dijk, Sr., whose skills as a photographer can hardly be equalled. Others who assisted him must accept some of that thanks, but it was his talent and most willing contributions of time that provided the bulk of the good photography for which I am grateful. For inspiration in a particular way, I acknowledge the interest and energy of Gary Lindstrom for his seasons of dedicated labor and his strong interests in all aspects of human history. He has proven that studies like this can be of as much interest to lay persons as to professional scholars and archeologists. Thanks are due to the few hundred volunteers and staff members who have sweat in the sun or labored in offices to accumulate and process the material that made this study possible. Chief among them, to my mind, is my own wife, Rita. For the frustrating tasks of assembling materials, typing and retyping, etc., I remain indebted to myself.

R. S. H.

Now as Josephus was thus engaged in the administration of the affairs of Galilee, there arose a treacherous person, a man of Gischala, the son of Levi, whose name was John. His character was that of a very cunning and very knavish person. . . . Poor he was at first, and for a long time his wants were a hinderance to him in his wicked designs. . . . However John's want of money had hitherto restrained him in his ambition after command, and in his attempts to advance himself. But when he saw that Josephus was highly pleased with the activity of his temper, he persuaded him, in the first place, to intrust him with the repairing of the walls of his native city, in which work he got a great deal of money from the rich citizens. He after that contrived a very shrewd trick, and pretending that the Jews who dwelt in Syria were obliged to make use of oil that was made by others than those of their own nation, he desired leave of Josephus to send oil to their borders; so he bought four amphorae with such Tyrian money as was of the value of four Attic drachmae, and sold every half amphorae at the same price. And as Galilee was very fruitful in oil, and was peculiarly so at that time, by sending away great quantities, and having the sole privilege so to do, he gathered an immense sum of money together, which money he immediately used to the disadvantage of him who gave him that privilege.

from *The Wars of the Jews*
by Josephus
as translated by William Whiston,
Chicago, 1902
Chap. 20, p. 582

# CHAPTER 1
# A REVIEW OF THE HISTORY OF TYRE

The history of Tyre has been well published. Wallace B. Fleming produced a study in 1915 that dealt with the classical sources and the archeological data known at the time. In 1969 Nina Jidejian updated Fleming's work with her handsomely illustrated work, *Tyre Through the Ages*, and finally, in 1973, H. Jacob Katzenstein published a detailed work covering the history of Tyre to the fall of the Neo-Babylonian empire.[1] For purposes of introducing the subject of Tyrian coinage I shall merely rehearse what has been pointed out more adequately by these and other authors.

The first mention of Tyre is from the Execration texts of the mid-19th century B.C.E. (Katzenstein 1973: 19). After a gap of some 500 years, next mention is in Ugaritic materials and the Amarna Letters of the 14th century B.C.E. Like other cities of the Levant at that time, it was vassal to Egypt and engaged in petty wars with rival states, if not harrassment from nomadic people.[2] There is reason to respect the ancient sources that testify to the antiquity of the site. Not that it was a notably large city from earliest times, of course, but that it did exist with some importance.

In a letter from one Egyptian official named *Hori* to another named *Amen-em-Opet*, we read a proud and instructive geographical account in which the following comment is made concerning Tyre: "They say another town is in the sea, named Tyre-the-Port. Water is taken to it by the boats, and it is richer in fish than the sands" (Pritchard 1955: 477). This assures us that the site was known to be on the island rather than the mainland but that its commerce and wealth may have been limited to the catching and selling of fish. We are reminded immediately of the fact that Tyrian fishermen were present at the gates and in the market of Jerusalem in the time of Nehemiah (Neh 13:15-22).

We are not sure of the actual effect of the Philistine invasion on the people and the site of Tyre. They may have been passed by, they may have endured siege or succumbed to it, or they may have absorbed some of the newcomers into their population. As confessed by Fleming (1915: 8, 14), a paucity of evidence precludes a conclusion. Both Justin and Josephus indicate that the city was founded ca. 1200 B.C.E. Could this refer to a refounding that should be connected with the founding of the mainland portion of the city? For Katzenstein, coin evidence from Sidon indicates a refounding by Sidonian refugees (1973: 59-62). What is both evident and important is the fact that Tyre grew and became a powerful city-state in the centuries that immediately followed.

It is listed as one of the important fortified cities of the time of Joshua (Josh 19:29), and there is evidence of its colonial activities in the westernmost parts of the Mediterranean at the time of King David.[3] In the biblical accounts of the United Kingdom of David and Solomon we get our first full view of the wealth and importance of the place. For the building of the new royal palace in Jerusalem, Hiram of Tyre provided cedar wood, carpenters, and masons

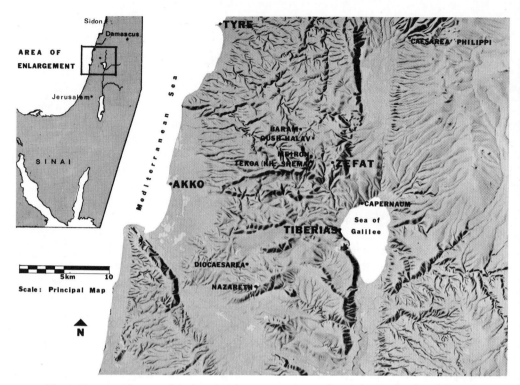

Fig. 1. Topographic map of Galilee showing excavated areas in relation to the city of Tyre.

(2 Sam 5:11). For the Temple, during the reign of Solomon, a skillful worker in bronze—also named Hiram according to the source—was added to the loan of craftsmen and supplies for the project. Supplies included cypress timber and gold. The Tyrians were capable providers of diverse commodities, and when the building project was finished, they teamed up with Solomon for a trade venture on the Red Sea (1 Kgs 5:1-18, 7:13-50, 9:11-14, 26-28). Already they had earned the reputation for trade and skill that would long endure.

In the century that followed the breakup of Solomon's kingdom, the alliance with the Phoenicians was inherited by Israel, the northern kingdom. In noting the marriage of Ahab to Jezebel, however, the writers of Kings call her "the daughter of Ethbaal, king of the Sidonians" (1 Kgs 16:31). Does this mean that Sidon was then dominant over Tyre or that Tyre was queen of all Phoenician cities and Sidonian was merely the term for Phoenician? The general consensus of scholars has for some time been in favor of the latter alternative (see Fleming 1915: 25; Kapelrud 1962a: 343-45; 1962b: 721-23; cf. Katzenstein 1973: 131).

There was a time in history that was Assyria's time. As did many other nations and states of that era, Tyre paid dearly for the Assyrians' greed. When

Tiglathpileser I (1114-1076 B.C.E.) reached the "Upper Sea toward the West," he received tribute from Byblos, Sidon, and Arvad but did not mention the name of Tyre (Pritchard 1955: 275). Likely he did not venture that far south. It is in the annals of Ashur-nasirpal II (883-859 B.C.E.) that Tyre is first named among the victims of Assyrian aggression. The "tribute of the seacoast," of Tyre, Sidon, Byblos, Mahallata, Maiza, Kaiza, Amurru, and Arvad was listed as "gold, silver, tin, copper, containers, linen garments with multicolored trimmings, large and small monkeys, ebony, boxwood" and "ivory" (Pritchard 1955: 276). The Phoenician cities were great centers of trade for commodities from the west and from Africa. Shalmaneser III (852-824 B.C.E.) also received tribute from Tyre, some of it "on ships" (Pritchard 1955: 280-81), as did Tiglathpileser III (744-727 B.C.E.; Pritchard 1955: 282). In the reports of Sennacherib (704-681 B.C.E.), however, it is Ushu, the mainland settlement, rather than Tyre that is listed among the "strong cities" that were "overwhelmed" (Pritchard 1955: 287). Did Tyre hold out too firmly against the conqueror? It is important to notice that up to that point the Tyrians had done no more than pay tribute. And it is also important to note that in spite of the harrassment from the Assyrians, the city's most famous western colony, Carthage, was founded during that period of time. The traditional date for that is 814 B.C.E. (see Harden 1962: 66-67; Moscati 1968: 114-17; Katzenstein 1973: 125).[4] Tyre was by no means a weak state during the time of Assyrian aggression. Tyrian trade westward hardly was hampered by the invasions and likely was welcomed by the Assyrians for what they could gain from it either through plunder or taxation.

In the reign of Esarhaddon (680-669 B.C.E.) the island city may have suffered injury. In an early campaign the Assyrian king boasts that he "conquered Tyre which is amidst the sea" (Pritchard 1955: 290), and on a text known as Prism B we read the following: "[Baᵓlu, king of Ty]re, living [on an island amidst the sea] . . . threw off my yoke . . . [of As]hur and the splendor of my lordship [overwhelmed him] . . . [he] bowed down and implored me, as his lord. . . . heavy [tribu]te, his daughters with dowries [as well as] all the [tribu]tes which he had omitted (to send). He kissed my feet. I took away from him those of his towns (which are situated on) the mainland [and re]organized [the region] turning it over to Assyria" (Pritchard 1955: 291).

It is worthy of note that Tyre had managed to "throw off the yoke" and gain control of the towns of the mainland as early as this. Such was the city's strength, in fact, that a prolonged siege was necessary in order to subdue its rulers and citizenry (Pritchard 1955: 292). It is nowhere said that the island-city was destroyed, and in the reign of the very next Assyrian king, Ashurbanipal (668-633 B.C.E.), a repeat performance of the same submission is recorded. Again, I quote the ancient source: "In my third campaign I marched against Baᵓil, king of Tyre, who lives (on an island) amidst the sea, because he did not heed my royal order, did not listen to my personal commands. I surrounded him with redoubts, seized his communications on sea and land. I (thus) intercepted and made scarce their food supply and forced them to submit to my yoke. He brought his own daughter and the daughters of his brothers before me to do menial services. At the same time, he brought his son Iahimilk who had not (yet) crossed the sea to greet me as (my) slave. I received from him his daughter and the daughters of his brothers with their great dowries. I had mercy upon him and returned to him the son, the offspring of his loins" (Pritchard 1955: 295-96).

This was the low point in Tyre's entire series of encounters with the Assyrians. Yet even here we may notice that the island itself was not penetrated. Baʾil *brought* his daughters, his nieces, and his son across the channel to the Assyrian king. Otherwise why should it be said that the son had "not yet crossed the sea"? They must have been forced to surrender because the food supply was cut off, not because the walls were breached. In regard to supplies of food and water the island was vulnerable. Otherwise its location was secure. That unique location plus its growing tradition of trade and skill made it the stronghold that it was. Tyre recovered swiftly to a position of wealth and influence as soon as Assyrian power weakened.[5]

The fate of Tyre during the time of neo-Babylonian power is less clear than we would like. Tyre was clearly caught between the Egyptians, in whose land Tyrian citizens actually lived, and the westward-expanding Babylonians. In one of the texts of Nebuchadnezzar, the king of Tyre is listed among rulers that were apparently subdued or made vassals (Pritchard 1955: 308). Josephus knew a source that said, "This king (Nebuchadnezzar) besieged Tyre thirteen years, while at the same time Ethbaal was king of Tyre" (*Ag. Ap.* 1.21; Josephus quoted Philostratus). The biblical evidence lends some support to this if one supposes that the oracles of Ezekiel were actual descriptions of the siege and if one reads Zedekiah for Jehoiakim in Jer 27:3, 12 or omits v. 1 with the LXX as Fleming did. Fleming took Josephus' source to be reliable and supposed that the mainland portion of the city fell while the island offered token submission (1915: 42-47), and Katzenstein has agreed with this, though with much more detailed evidence to support it (1973: 330-33). With the king in exile, however, judges were appointed to govern the city (Katzenstein 1973: 337). Whatever actually happened, we do have from this time a most marvelous portrayal of pre-Alexandrian Tyre from the Book of Ezekiel. Because of the importance of its details, I quote a goodly portion of it.

> O Tyre, you have said, "I am perfect in beauty."
> Your borders are in the heart of the seas;
> your builders made perfect your beauty.
> They made all your planks of fir trees from Senir;
> they took a cedar from Lebanon to make a mast for you.
> Of oaks of Bashan they made your oars;
> they made your deck of pines from the coasts of Cyprus, inlaid with ivory.
> Of fine embroidered linen from Egypt was your sail, serving as your ensign;
> blue and purple from the coasts of Elishah was your awning.
> The inhabitants of Sidon and Arvad were your rowers;
> skilled men of Zemer were in you, they were your pilots.
> The elders of Gebal and her skilled men were in you, caulking your seams;
> all the ships of the sea with their mariners were in you, to barter for your wares.
>
> Persia and Lud and Put were in your army as your men of
> war; they hung the shield and helmet in you; they gave

you splendor. The men of Arvad and Helech were upon your
walls round about, and men of Gamad were in your towers;
they hung their shields upon your walls round about; they
made perfect your beauty.

Tarshish trafficked with you because of your great wealth
of every kind; silver, iron, tin, and lead they exchanged
for your wares. Javan, Tubal and Meshech traded with you;
they exchanged the persons of men and vessels of bronze
for your merchandise. Beth-togarmah exchanged for your
wares horses, war horses, and mules. The men of Rhodes
traded with you; many coastlands were your own special
markets, they brought you in payment ivory tusks and ebony.
Edom trafficked with you because of your abundant goods;
they exchanged for your wares emeralds, purple, embroidered
work, fine linen, coral, and agate. Judah and the land
of Israel traded with you; they exchanged for your
merchandise wheat, olives and early figs, honey, oil and
balm. Damascus trafficked with you for your abundant
goods, because of your great wealth of every kind; wine
of Helbon, and white wool, and wine from Uzal they exchanged
for your wares; wrought iron, cassia, and calamus were
bartered for your merchandise. Dedan traded with you in
saddlecloths for riding. Arabia and all the princes of
Kedar were your favored dealers in lambs, rams, and goats;
in these they trafficked with you. The traders of Sheba
and Raamah traded with you; they exchanged for your wares
the best of all kinds of spices, and all precious stones,
and gold. Haran, Canneh, Eden, Asshur, and Chilmad traded
with you. These traded with you in choice garments, in
clothes of blue and embroidered work, and in carpets of
colored stuff, bound with cords and made secure; in these
they traded with you. The ships of Tarshish traveled for
you with your merchandise.

So you were filled and heavily laden in the heart of the seas.

(Ezek 27:3-25, RSV)

. . . by your wisdom and your understanding
you have gotten wealth for yourself,
and have gathered gold and silver into your treasuries;
by your great wisdom in trade you have increased your wealth,
and your heart has become proud in your wealth. . . .

(Ezek 28:4-5, RSV)

Under the Persians Tyre enjoyed the same degree of autonomy as that of
her neighbors. The city was part of the fifth satrapy, which included Cyprus as
well as the rest of the Levant. There were taxes to be paid to the Persian
government, but there was freedom of commerce that no doubt brought
prosperity to the city and its territories. At the beginning of Persian rule, at
least, there was building and a new demand for the building supplies of the

Phoenician coast. Economic recovery must have been relatively rapid. Facilitating that and in the context of it, coins were struck in imitation of that which had already been done by the Greeks and the Lydians in the west.[6] According to commonly accepted sources, the first coins of Tyre were struck somewhere toward the end of the 5th century B.C.E.

Together with the other Phoenician cities, Tyre was forced to provide naval forces for the Persians in their efforts at westward expansion into the lands of the Greeks. We know that Phoenicians were able to act in concert at that time for it was then that Tyre, Sidon, and Aradus formed the new city of Tripoli where they had a common council. We do not know what percentage of the fleet was specifically Tyrian. We only know that they were part of it and that, in turn, would matter when the tides of power would one day reverse and Hellenistic armies would move eastward.

According to Diodorus there was a war between the Persians and a certain Evagorus of Cyprus that began in the year 392 B.C.E. This Evagorus had assassinated the Tyrian ruler of Cyprus, one Abdemon by name. Athenian and Egyptian fleets came to the aid of the rebel. According to Isocrates, the Egyptians took Tyre by assault, and as a result Tyre provided the Egyptian fleet with 20 triremes. Ten years later the rebellion was subdued and Tyre was once again under full control of the Persians (Fleming 1915: 52-53).

Late in the 4th century B.C.E. came the disaster that could match the prophetic predictions that had been made by the Jewish prophet Ezekiel (Ezekiel 27-29). Alexander's siege of Tyre was the single most glorious and tragic event in the known history of the island city. The conqueror's proud determination and military ingenuity were more than matched by the ingenuity and courage of the Tyrian defenders. Relying upon aid from their great daughter-city, Carthage, they sent their children and elders there for refuge as soon as they understood that the Macedonian would not settle for a token surrender of the city. Alexander had no fleet. Therefore, he set his engineers and laborers to the task of constructing the mole that still joins the one-time island to the coast today. The Tyrians disrupted that attempt repeatedly, and when it was completed, it was not that alone, but also the aid of a fleet from Cyprus, that made it possible for Alexander to breach the city. Aid for the Tyrians from Carthage never came. It was destroyed and 2,000 crucified soldiers of Tyre were posted as sentinels over the ruins (Fleming 1915: 54-64).

But the recovery of Tyre was fully as remarkable as the siege. The siege, seven months in duration, ended in July of the year 332 B.C.E. Soon after that, refugees returned and new colonists settled in with them (see Fleming 1915: 64-65).[7] Within 18 years Tyre once again became a city to be reckoned with among the other venerable Phoenician cities: so much to be reckoned with, in fact, that Tyre was honored with another siege—of 15 months this time—that ended in 312 as Ptolemy struggled with Antigonus for the territories of Cyprus and Phoenicia. The Ptolemies gained and held control of this area until 198 B.C.E., when it passed back into the hands of the Seleucid kings. From the time preceding 198 we have a series of coins from there that were minted by the Ptolemies. After that date, Tyre became an important Seleucid mint.[8]

Our earliest available archeological evidence gives us some indication of the architecture and culture of the city during the period of Hellenization. The first excavations were conducted by Ernst Renan in 1860 and were resumed in 1903 by the curator of the Imperial Museum at Constantinople. In 1921 a survey was made by a French mission, and in 1934-36 an aerial survey and sea-diving expedition were conducted by A. Poidebard, S. J. Emir Maurice Chéhab began excavations there in 1947 that have not yet been concluded (see Jidejian 1969: xi, xviii). The evidence from these excavations indicates that the site was quite thoroughly Hellenized. Indeed, we cannot be sure how much of the population was Greek or of other foreign elements vis-à-vis its old Phoenician stock. It is also hard to assess the city's strength in contrast to former times, but it is safe to say that it was by no means an unimportant city in political terms and that it continued to be influential as a center of commerce (see Fleming 1915: 66-67; cf. Kapelrud 1962b: 723). In the great struggle between Rome and Carthage in the west, Tyre was either not able or not willing to give actual aid—likely for reasons of its subordination to Seleucid rule as much as military impotence—but very willing to receive Hannibal as a refugee when he fled there by ship in 201 B.C.E. According to Pliny he was received with honor (Fleming 1915: 67). Soon thereafter, Hannibal persuaded the Seleucid ruler, Antiochus III, to go to war against Rome. Hannibal was made an admiral of the Phoenician fleet but performed poorly at it. The Seleucid forces were driven out of Greece and parts of Asia Minor and were forced to humiliating terms of peace in 187 B.C.E.

A Jewish impression of the city from those times is given to us in 2 Macc 4:18-20 where we read, "When the quadrennial games were being held at Tyre and the king was present, the vile Jason sent envoys, chosen as being Antiochian citizens from Jerusalem, to carry three hundred silver drachmas for the sacrifice to Herakles. Those who carried the money, however, thought best not to use it for sacrifice, because that was inappropriate, but to expend it for another purpose. So this money was intended by the sender for the sacrifice to Herakles, but by the decision of its carrier it was applied to the construction of triremes." A number of things are apparent here. One is the importance of Tyre in the eyes of the Seleucid government. Another is the identification of the venerable Melqart with the Greek Herakles, an identification that goes back to Alexander himself. Most important of all, Tyre was still a center of shipbuilding and naval skills. When ruled by others, Tyrian skills as well as Tyrian commercial tradition were of value to those who were privileged to exercise that rule.

In the year 126/5 B.C.E. the Tyrians were granted permission to issue autonomous coins. What other privileges were granted in connection with this we cannot tell, for none of the sources tell us. Only this fact stands as an intriguing detail.[9] Whatever the degree of autonomy vis-à-vis the Syrians, Tyre and the rest of Phoenicia endured the control of Tigranes of Armenia from 83 until 69 B.C.E., and then a brief resurgence of Seleucid power "freed" them from that until the arrival of the Romans.

Roman sources speak of the independence of the city, and the continued coinage of the independent era reinforces that. What is difficult to assess is the degree of that independence. Those same Roman sources inform us that Julius

Caesar removed the votive offerings of Herakles at Tyre because the Tyrians had harbored the wife and son of Pompey and that the Tyrians continued to support Pompey during that period of intra-Roman rivalries. Free or not free, they were one of the pawns in the great chess game of Roman power. Octavian disciplined them for their factious quarreling, and Josephus states that Mark Anthony was unable to present Tyre and Sidon to Cleopatra because he knew them to have been free cities from their ancestors (Fleming 1915: 70-71). They were also involved in the struggles that surrounded the Herodian dynasty (Jidejian 1969: 86-89). What was most vital of all to the life of the city, of course, was continued commerce. The evidence we have indicates that it thrived. Tyre continued to be one of the important trade cities of the Levant. Strabo, the Greek geographer of the 1st century, has left us a colorful image of the city that is well worth quoting.

> Tyre is wholly an island, being built up nearly in the same way as Aradus; and it is connected with the mainland by a mole, which was constructed by Alexander when he was besieging it; and it has two harbors, one that can be closed and the other, called "Aegyptian" harbor, open. The houses here, it is said, have many stories, even more than the houses of Rome, and on this account, when an earthquake took place, it lacked but little of utterly wiping out the city. The city was also unfortunate when it was taken siege by Alexander; but it overcame such misfortunes and restored itself both by means of the seamanship of its people, in which the Phoenicians in general have been superior to all people of all times, and by means of their dye houses for purple; for the Tyrian purple has proved itself by far the most beautiful of all; and the shellfish are caught near the coast; and the other things requisite for dyeing are easily got; and although the great number of dye-works makes the city unpleasant to live in, yet it makes the city rich through the superior skill of its inhabitants. The Tyrians were judged autonomous, not only by the kings, but also, at small expense to them, by the Romans, when the Romans confirmed the decree of the kings. Heracles is paid extravagant honors by them. The number and the size of their colonial cities is an evidence of their power in maritime affairs. Such, then, are the Tyrians (*Geography of Strabo* 16.2.23, quoted also by Jidejian 1969: xvii).

Pliny the Elder, by contrast, praises the historical role of the city but informs us that its renown in his day was limited to the trade of shellfish and a purple dye (*Natural History* 5.17.76, quoted also by Jidejian 1969: xvii). Certainly Tyre could no longer have been the grand mistress of the sea-lanes that was described so strikingly by the prophet Ezekiel. But neither was she nothing. The details we know from the 1st century suggest a bustling old seaport that still had commercial vitality and a considerable population for its size.

Early in the Roman period there was established at Sidon a school of philosophy. Two stoics of Tyre are mentioned among its members. More to the expertise of these Phoenicians, however, were the geographers whose ranks included Marinus of Tyre, a man who produced a map with mathematically constructed longitude and latitude early in the 2nd century. At that time a rhetorician known as Paulus of Tyre appeared before Emperor Hadrian to plead for the honor of his city. As a result, Tyre was granted the status of

Metropolis in the Roman Empire. The city seemingly had gained in sophistication some of what it had lost in commercial importance. In addition to that, the Christian church was firmly planted there in apostolic times (Acts 21:3-4), and the church there would eventually become the seat of a bishop.

The new rank of Metropolis is reflected in the coins. Those struck prior to that date bear such legends as TYPOY IEPAΣ KAI AΣYΛOY or abbreviations thereof. Following this elevation of the city's rank, the legends read MHTPOΠOΛEΩΣ or the longer formulae, IEPAC MHTPOΠOΛEΩC and TYPOY MHTPOΠOΛEΩC.[10]

In 192 C.E. Tyre once again reaped the ill fortunes of political power conflict. Septimius Severus and Pescennias Niger were rivals for the office of emperor. While Niger was still in control of much territory in the Levant, Tyre acted upon a report of his failure to stop the army of Severus at the passes of the Taurus and proclaimed Severus emperor in fact. Niger responded by sending troops to plunder the city. The city was burned, and some number of its citizens were slaughtered. But after Niger was defeated at Issus in 194 C.E., Severus rewarded the city for its loyalty to himself by giving it the title of Colony of Septimius to add to its former honor. The coins reflect this elevation with the reverse inscription, SEP TVRVS METR COLONI or variations of that (Jidejian 1969: 91). In a special way, the city was claimed by the emperor.

The archeological remains that represent the Roman period are fairly impressive. Both buildings and sarcophagi reveal a merging of Hellenistic and Roman influences in the architecture of the site. Descriptions of the city from those times indicate that it was a cosmopolitan place famous still for its purple dye industry, but also well known as a market for the selling of linen and a center for the manufacture of glass. For the Romans and others to the west, it was one of the doorways to the east. For the people in its own area, it was a center of trade and a wholesaler for Egyptian goods and other items from the west.

There were events in the 3rd century that most directly affected Tyre. There was a general persecution of Christians ordered by the emperor Decius in the years 250-57 C.E. In that persecution Origen was imprisoned and tortured at Tyre, according to Christian sources, and when the cathedral of Tyre was eventually built, its altar covered his body. We know of a bishop of Tyre named Marinus and an important opponent of Christianity named Porphyry ("clad in purple"; Fleming 1915: 74-75; Jidejian 1969: 91). He was a neoplatonist, and in 262 he went to Rome to join the school of Plotinus. One who responded to his attacks was Methodius, another bishop of Tyre.

During the reign of Diocletian (284-305) a certain Dorotheus found favor with the emperor and was honored by being placed at the head of the purple dye factories in the city. He was acquainted with "the most liberal studies and a Greek primary education" and was "by nature a eunuch" (Jacoby 1923). At that time there were bloody persecutions of Christians.

Roman history for the 3rd century is poorly documented. We know the names of the emperors, and we know some of the wars that they fought as they vied for power, but for some periods we know preciously little more than that.

It was a time when imperial lineage came to mean less and less while military skill and power meant more and more. Money suffered severe inflation. At the end of the century the emperor Diocletian undertook drastic measures to patch the leaks in what was beginning to look like a sinking ship. He announced new standards of gold and silver, but more important than that, he authorized the striking of huge quantities of thin coppers in small denominations that were mere tokens of value. The Roman Empire had over-extended itself. The costs of war in the never-ending struggles to hold the borders diminished the substance of its power.

In connection with this, interesting developments took place in the religion of the imperial rulers. It is safe to say that Roman republican religion survived only in small circles, and one must point out that already in the 1st century many religions, and chiefly those known as the mystery religions, made great inroads into the ruling class, the armies, and even some of the population at large. At the beginning of the 3rd century, however, we see a development that turned out to be of great political importance as the imperial family adopted the cult of Sol Invictus as the official religion of the rulers. The most drastic stride was taken by the most incapable of the emperors, the one who titled himself *Elagabalus*. Despite his political insufficiencies, the religion that he promoted held fast. As late as the time of Constantine the Great we see a series of coins with the reverse legend *soli invicto comiti* with the figure of the sun-god in the center. In the meantime, the images of the emperors on the obverses of the most common coins of the 3rd century, the *antoniani*, are depicted with the radiate crown of the sun on their heads. There were hints of the traditional Roman mythologies of the sun in the iconography, but for the most part, this was the conquest of the empire by the sun deity memorialized at Emesa in Syria whose chief priest and devotee had been the young emperor Bassanius, alias Elagabalus (see Halsberghe 1972; Seyrig 1971: 337-73; Tacitus *Hist.* 3.24-25).

## NOTES

[1]Fleming's work was titled *The History of Tyre* and was published as vol. 10 of the Columbia University Oriental Studies. It was reprinted by AMS Press, New York, in 1966. Jidejian's book, published in Beirut, is excellent in part because of her access to materials in the museums of that city. Katzenstein has leaned heavily on biblical sources and in that respect has complemented the work of the other two authors. The full title of his work, published in Jerusalem at Goldberg's Press, is *The History of Tyre from the Beginning of the Second Millennium B.C.E. until the Fall of the New-Babylonian Empire in 538 B.C.E.* All three sources are furnished with complete bibliographies.

[2]Katzenstein, following Albright (1973: 19-20), places credibility in the reading of "Tyre" for *ṣr-m* in *The Tale of Keret*. Fleming (1915: 8-12) had given a good analysis of the Abimilki letters (see Pritchard 1955: 484) that make mention of Tyre. The last note of correspondence we know of is a plea for wood and water. In an earlier letter we learn that a mere 20 additional soldiers (or companies?) were required to hold the city against besiegers. This would indicate that the site was not of colossal proportions.

[3]Katzenstein has pointed out, quite wisely, that Abibaal's pact with David was for the purpose of containing the Philistines. Fleming, in 1915, claimed that there is evidence of Tyre's colonial activities in the westernmost parts of the Mediterranean as early as 1100 B.C.E. More recently, D. Harden has concluded, "Indeed, if we are wise we shall not push any Phoenician colonies back behind 1000 and will be chary of accepting even a tenth-century date for any colony in the west" (1962: 64). Katzenstein concurs with this latter opinion and sees the 10th century as the beginning of Tyre's new era of strength and expansion. On the mainland, that expansion reached south to Mt. Carmel, and Solomon's fortification of Megiddo defended the Israelite border. Yet, in juxtaposition to this, Katzenstein has pointed out the evidence for building skills with trimmed megaliths that could only reach back several centuries (1973: 75, 91-114).

[4]This entire period is discussed in excellent detail by Katzenstein in that he points out the shorter periods of ebb and flow in Assyrian power and the conflicts of power within Tyre itself, notably that of king and populace versus the aristocracy as led by the priests of Melqart. While there were regular payments of tribute to Assyria, Tyre continued to hold the coastal territories to the south as well as expanding her power in Cyprus and farther west. There, in the Mediterranean, she was rivalled by the Greeks. In a concluding statement, Katzenstein has said, "Tyre, in remaining an independent state, became a valuable source of income to the Assyrians" (1973: 212).

[5]The Yavneh-Yam letters and 2 Kings 22-23 indicate that Judah did so. How much more must have been the comeback of Tyre. Katzenstein points out that Tyre remained neutral in the wars that accompanied the fall of Assyria while being careful to regain all its former territories on the mainland and becoming once again the leading city on the Phoenician coast (1973: 276-98). Katzenstein has also given due attention to the struggles in the west, where Tyre and Carthage had to compete with land-hungry Greeks in their efforts to maintain their trading centers and their access to raw materials (1973: 276).

[6]Until recently there was a tendency to accept far too early a date for the beginning of coinage. Philip Grierson (1975: 10) gives us the studied opinion that the earliest date is somewhere between 550 and 530 B.C.E.

[7]E. T. Newell (1923: 1) claims that the city was totally reinhabited by Carians who were brought in by Alexander. Because I see too many signs of old Phoenician skills as well as the presence of native Tyrian symbols on the coins from succeeding periods, I cannot agree with Newell.

[8]According to Newell (1923: 1) the Ptolemaic issues in Tyre itself began at about 306 B.C.E. and were preceded by a mint at Acre, which struck coins for use at Tyre as early as 321 B.C.E.; Tyre itself seems to have been in Seleucid hands earlier than 198. Newell (1936: 1-2) also dates Seleucid issues from Tyre as early as 201 B.C.E.

[9]Moscati (1968: 27) has challenged the date, claiming that the year should be 120 B.C.E. His arguments are not apparent, for he has given no explanations for this and presents no evidence.

[10]The form of Greek *sigma* shifted from $\Sigma$ to C during the 1st and 2nd centuries. This can be a factor in determining whether coins are early or late in that period.

# CHAPTER 2
# COINAGE AT TYRE TO THE END OF THE
# 2ND CENTURY C.E.

Although coins had been in use in the eastern part of the Mediterranean since as early as the late 6th century B.C.E. (Grierson 1975: 10), the Phoenician cities generally were not striking their own until the 3rd century. Sidon and Tyre anticipated this with coins from as early as the end of the 5th century B.C.E.

Those first coins of Tyre are silver staters of a weight approaching 14 grams when in good condition. The iconography of the obverse is true to the maritime functions of the city, for it consists of a dolphin swimming to the right over a triple line of waves with a murex shell below (fig. 2). The murex shell betokens the trade in purple dye for which the city was long famous. On the reverse of the coin we see an owl with its body set to our right and its face turned toward us. Behind the owl, as though clasped by the wing that we cannot see, are two symbols familiar to us from the accouterments of ancient Egyptian pharaohs: a flail and a crook (fig. 3; see Hill 1965: 227; pl. 26).[1] This motif of the owl, taken from Attic coins, indicates the extent of Attic influence in that area, but the style is not Greek. The owl has more the proportions and stance of an old Egyptian hieroglyph, but more important than that, the added symbols show us that the Tyrians were not able to accept the owl as a sufficient symbol of authority. It had to be supplemented by the two more ancient symbols of Egyptian royal authority, the flail and the crook. Old Phoenician trade habits had developed a strong affinity for things Egyptian, an affinity also manifested in the art and iconography of the Tyrian colonial city Carthage. Fractions of this coin with the same design were issued at 1/4 and 1/24 in silver.

The next series of coins, dated by G. F. Hill to the period 400-332 B.C.E. (1965: 229-30), is also of silver and based on the same weights and fractions thereof. The iconography has changed radically on the obverse. In the place of the dolphin is Melqart, "Lord of the City," astride the back of a hippocamp (a horse with wings and the tail of a sea creature) that is carrying him to the viewer's right. There are two lines to represent waves beneath. The dolphin is subordinated to a position below that. The murex shell is absent. The reverse is essentially the same as that of the first series, with the owl and its crook and flail, but letters and numerals have been added. The letters are the Phoenician *mem* (𐤌) and, in some instances, the *bet* (𐤁; Hill 1965: 229; pls. 28-29).

It is reasonable to guess that the *mem* stood for *mina*, a Semitic name for a weight, except that a mina represented about 500 grams and that is far too heavy for these coins which range up to little more than 13 grams in weight. Vertical marks are sometimes found in place of (or in addition to) the letters, yet in all cases the weight of the coin is approximately the same. The *bet* seems a mystery, unless it stands for *ba$^c$al*. Perhaps the *mem* even stands for *Melqart*. The strokes are most obviously numerals, with a stroke representing 1, a crescent representing 10 and a double crescent, 20. The numbers may indicate dates, but with no known point of reference we cannot place them on any

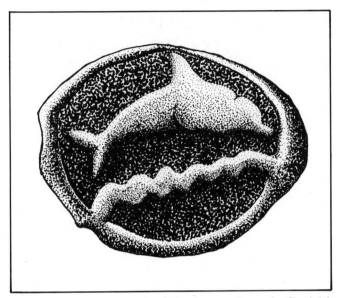

Fig. 2. The dolphin as seen on a coin of 450-400 B.C.E. Drawn by Carol Adamac.

calendar (see Hill 1965: 229, 231-32; cf. Newell 1923: 16, 21). A circle occurs in connection with some of the strokes. The occasional presence of the letter *ṣade* (𐤑) seems to be clear, for that would seem to abbreviate the name of the city itself. In light of that I must conclude that the letters *mem* and *bet mem* must signify Melqart and Baal Melqart, the most obvious of all possibilities.

The figure of Melqart on the strange sea-creature recalls the Ugaritic cycle of texts concerning the great struggle between the primeval God of the Storm and *Yamm*, the Sea. Here we seem to have the old Canaanite Rider of the Clouds in a seagoing version as Rider of the Waves. Yet the whole idea seems strongly Greek, for it was in Greece that Poseidon was associated with the horse, and winged horses were a common motif.

Our chief source for the coins of the Ptolemaic era is the study done by E. T. Newell (1923). To introduce the subject we quote from Newell's introduction (1923: 1-2).

> During this period an active local trade must have sprung up between the inhabitants of the city, those of the mainland, and the large garrisons maintained in the fortress by Alexander and his successors. Evidence of this exists in the copper coins which as early as the year 321 B.C. had to be struck at Ake for use in Tyre. These coins, while bearing the letters TY, initials of the name of Tyre, were certainly struck at Ake, as proved by their style, the name of that mint in Phoenician letters 𐤕𐤊 , and the accompanying date—regnal year of the local dynast. . . . The important point of all this for us lies in the incontrovertible evidence these copper coins present, that at least as late as the year 321-20 B.C., no mint had as yet been re-established at Tyre. . . . Apparently the state of affairs as outlined . . . continued for another twelve years or so. Then eventually a mint was re-opened at Tyre, never to be closed again until the reign of the Roman emperor Gallienus, more than half a millenium later.

Fig. 3. The Tyrian owl as seen on a coin of 302 B.C.E. Drawn by Carol Adamac.

Compared to the coins that were struck prior to the conquest of Alexander, the shift in iconography is radical. The following types comprise the coins of this era.

1. A tetradrachma (ca. 17 g) with the bust of Herakles in a lion headdress on the obverse. On the reverse, Zeus is seated on a throne with an eagle perched on his outstretched right arm while his left hand grasps the top of a long sceptre. Beneath the eagle we see the monogram ⟨symbol⟩ and beneath the throne, the monogram ⟨symbol⟩ . At the right, reading from the top is the legend ΑΛΕΞΑΝΔΡΟΥ.

2. A stater (ca. 8.60 g) with the bust of Athena in a Corinthian helmet adorned with a double-coiled serpent on the obverse. On the reverse, winged Nike is standing with a wreath in her outstretched right arm, her left arm holding a long stylus. In the left field is the monogram ⟨symbol⟩, in the right field, ⟨symbol⟩. At the right, reading from the top, is the legend ΑΛΕΞΑΝΔΡΟΥ.

The two coins above represent the first series, which Newell dated to 306-301 B.C.E. A second series, dating from 301 to 290, includes both types but with small differences in detail. On the reverse of the tetradrachma we see the addition of the title ΒΑΣΙΛΕΩΣ in the exergue of some of the coins, and in the field position beneath the eagle, a war club within a circle in place of a monogram. This club within a circle appears also on some staters.

The club within a circle is a regular feature on a third series, dated to the years 290-287 B.C.E., that is otherwise like the preceding except that on some tetradrachmas we see ΔΗΜΗΤΡΙΟΥ in place of ΑΛΕΞΑΝΔΡΟΥ. The year 286 B.C.E. marks the beginning of Ptolemaic issues and the appearance of a new type.

3. The Ptolemaic tetradrachma is smaller, weighing slightly more than 14 g. On the obverse is the bust of Ptolemy Soter with a laureate band about his head. On the reverse is an eagle facing to our left, perched on a thunderbolt. In the field at the left we see either a small dolphin or a war club. Reading around from bottom left and continuing from top right is the legend ΒΑΣΙΛΕΩΣ ΠΤΟΛΕΜΑΙΟΥ.

Newell noted that by this time the mints of Sidon and of Acco had both ceased to produce coins and that during the reign of Ptolemy Soter and the first years of Philadelphus, Tyre was the sole producer in the Phoenician area. Ptolemaic issues ceased at about 201 B.C.E., after which Tyre served as a minting center for Antiochus III and his successors.

Still within the Ptolemaic period we see the reappearance of an old, local Tyrian coin in the form of an Attic didrachma with Melqart riding the hippocamp on the obverse and the owl with flail and crook on the reverse. Newell delineated three groups of these: (a) one with the letter *ṣade* and the date numerals ||, |||, or ||||, (b) one bearing the letters *mem* and *bet* or the letter *mem* followed by the numbers |, ||, or |||, and (c) a group bearing dates from 23 to 37.[2]

The city of Tyre served as a mint for the Seleucid kings from the reign of Antiochus III to the reign of Demetrius II or, in dates, from 201 to 125 B.C.E. (Newell 1921, 1936; Rogers 1927). Silver coins were issued in four denominations: the tetradrachma, the didrachma, the drachma, and the half drachma. In an initial series, lasting from 201 to 151 B.C.E., the standard is Attic with a tetradrachma weighing 17.40 g. After that date until 125 B.C.E., the Egyptian standard was followed with the tetradrachma weighing 14.20 g, a factor which may mean that the chief trading interest was maritime and with Egypt (Rogers 1927: 5). Copper coins were issued also in four denominations that we know as the chalkous, the hemichalkous, the dilepton, and the lepton, with weights of ca. 8, 4, 2, and 1 g respectively.

All coins in this group feature the bust of the emperor on the obverse, pictured with a slim diadem about the head and always facing to our right. Around the circumference is a neat circle of dots. On the reverses of the silver coins we see Apollo, sitting on an omphalos and holding a bow and arrow. The Tyrian war club in the left field is the mark of the city. The legend reads vertically on two sides, ΒΑΣΙΛΕΩΣ ΑΝΤΙΟΧΟΥ, ΒΑΣΙΛΕΩΣ ΣΕΛΕΥΚΟΥ or ΒΑΣΙΛΕΩΣ ΑΝΤΙΟΧΟΥ ΘΕΟΥ ΕΠΙΦΑΝΟΥ ΝΙΚΗΦΟΡΟΥ. In 150 B.C.E. the reverses change to depict an eagle standing toward left on the spur of a galley with a palm branch over its right shoulder. In right field is a date place over a monogram. In left field, a club is surmounted with the monogram of Tyre. A smaller number from the late period picture Zeus enthroned and facing left with his left arm resting on a sceptre. Alongside the Tyrian club is the inscribed word ΙΕΡΑΣ, in two parts. On such coins of Demetrius II the full title of the monarch reads ΒΑΣΙΛΕΩΣ ΔΗΜΗΤΡΙΟΥ ΘΕΟΥ ΝΙΚΑΤΟΡΟΣ.

The striking feature of this group is the totally Greek character of the iconography. These are not truly Tyrian coins. They are coins of the Greek rulers minted at Tyre. By contrast, the bronze coins of the Seleucid period bear

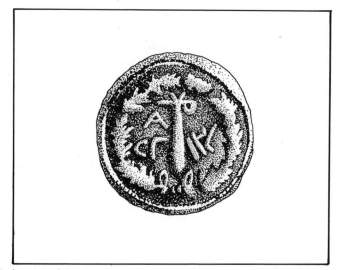

Fig. 4. The Tyrian club of Heracles with the city's monogram at the top as seen on a coin of 77/8 C.E. Drawn by Carol Adamac.

local iconography on the reverse. The largest denomination in bronze, the chalkous, features the stern of a galley that is usually ornamented with the amphlaston. The date, in Greek letters, appears above. The hemichalkous features the prow of a galley and a palm or a dolphin swimming downward. The inscriptional material for both of these coins includes the name and title of the king, the city's name as ΤΥΡΙΩΝ, and at the bottom of the coin, *lṣr* ("of Tyre") and *ᵓm ṣdnm* ("mother of the Sidonians"). There are relatively few hemichalkoi, which must mean that relatively few of that denomination were struck (Newell 1936: 24).

The dilepton features a palm tree with hanging fruit on the reverse. ΒΑΣΙΛΕΩΣ plus the name of the monarch is written around. The date is in the center and is divided by the trunk of the palm tree (see pls. 1-2 for our examples). The lepton, which is sparsely represented, has the war club of Tyrian Herakles on the reverse. The king's name and title are written around as on the dilepton. The date was apparently written across the field of the coin.

The palm tree was a symbol that would become quite standard among cities of the Levant. Apparently, it was the local conception of the tree of life. Depictions of a galley bear witness to Tyre's proud maritime history. The club of Herakles shows Greek influence, of course, but we have already noted that the exploits of Phoenician Baal Melqart were equated with those of the Greek Herakles. Baal Melqart and Herakles merged quite easily in the minds of both Greek and native. Such iconography as that seen in these examples demonstrates the degree of autonomy enjoyed by the city during this period of coinage. The autonomous period which followed was not all that radical a break, for the bronze coins done under Seleucid rule were already quite local in character.

Autonomous coinage officially began in 126/5 B.C.E., and it continued into Roman times through the period when Tyre was given the title Metropolis until the end of the 2nd century C.E. Autonomy is demonstrated on these coins by the absence of any royal or imperial image on the obverse. The iconography is Tyrian or native to the Levant, although some of the symbols are Hellenized. The elements used include the Phoenician galley, a goddess in the guise of Tyche with a turreted crown on her head, the date palm, the bust of Melqart—quite thoroughly Greek in appearance,[3] the Heraklean war club within an oak wreath, and late in the series, the temple of the Phoenician Koinon. An early series continues the Ptolemaic eagle for a time. Various series overlap in time.

Earliest are a silver shekel and a half-shekel with the bust of Melqart, slightly whiskered and laureate-crowned, on the obverse. A lion skin is knotted around his neck, and a circle of dots encloses the image. On the reverse, an eagle stands facing to our left, his right foot on the beak of a ship and a palm branch over his right shoulder. In the left side of the field is the date in Greek numerals and a war club suspended downward. Written around the circumference, from right downward, is the inscription ΤΥΡΟΥ ΙΕΡΑΣ ΚΑΙ ΑΣΥΛΟΥ. Hill (1965: 233-53; pls. 29-31) noted that this type was minted from 126/5 B.C.E. to 65/6 C.E. The weight of the shekel is up to 14.50 g, the half-shekel, up to 7.25 g.

The eagle, hearkening back to Ptolemaic authority, seems to declare that Tyre had preferred the Ptolemaic to the Seleucid regime. Or is this just another example of an affinity for things Egyptian? The war club was apparently felt to be truly Tyrian, for it would replace the eagle as the dominant insignia on the reverse when the silver issues gave way to large coppers. The palm leaf over the shoulder of the eagle is an element of a symbol that must have been felt to be very powerful throughout the Levant, for it figured on many coins of many cities and provinces. The prow of the galley represents a tenacious Phoenician tradition. Despite the dominance of the eagle on the series of silver coins, all the subordinate symbols testify to a particular Tyrian pride. The inclusion of ΙΕΡΑΣ and ΑΣΥΛΟΥ is the assertion of something like an actual title for the city. "The sacred and inviolate City of Tyre" is the full import of the legend.

Early in this period, prior to 55/4 B.C.E. at least, is a bronze type with Melqart on the obverse and a palm tree with the inscription ΙΕΡΑΣ on the reverse. Hill (1965: 254; pl. 31:5) has given but one example of this coin weighing 2.07 g. It is dated HK (28), which is 99/8 B.C.E. In our excavations at Meiron we unearthed one example of this type (M74 100 on p. 57 below).

A very important type of bronze coin was begun by a series that lasted from 55/4 B.C.E. to 86/7 C.E. The obverse features the bust of Melqart. On the reverse is an oak wreath and the club with the Tyrian monogram atop. On some coins the club alone can be taken as a Tyrian symbol, but this special form of the club is predominant. In the field, to left and to right, is a date and the letters *lṣr* (belonging to Tyre) in Phoenician characters (Hill 1965: 257; pl. 31: 10; see pls. 6-8 for our examples).

At this point it is necessary to backtrack and look at the beginning of another set of motifs on a series of bronze coins. The symbol on the obverses of these coins is the turreted bust of Tyche. Tyche-Fortuna, with her headdress of turreted towers, was the protectress of many cities of the Levant, most notably of Antioch (see Liddell and Scott 1940: 1839). One could suppose that it was a Seleucid symbol and therefore a trace of Seleucid authority in the autonomous coinage of Tyre, but a survey of Seleucid coins forecloses that. This is the Levantine depiction of the city goddess, and as such, it may tie into many old myths and legends of local goddesses. Both the providence and fate of a city were represented by this figure. This was a city's claim to and hope for good luck. Quite likely no city's existence was complete without a figure of this sort or its equivalent. The palm branch that generally appears behind her is a unique feature of the Tyrian Tyche and a hint of the symbol that appears on the reverses of the earliest series of this type—a small bronze coin with a simple palm tree bearing two clusters of dates. A ring of dots neatly encircles the figure. The weights vary from 0.34 to 1.53 g (Hill 1965: 253). There is no way to give them an exact date. Hill has suggested "toward the end of the Second Cent. B.C."

Succeeding this, if Hill's dates are correct, is a series that dates from 108/7 to 65/4 B.C.E. The obverse is the same as that of the coin above, but the reverse is expanded to include "L" plus a date and IEP$^{A}$A$\overset{\smallsmile}{\Sigma}$ which must be a schematized abbreviation for IEPAΣ AΣYΛOY, in the field with *lṣr* in Phoenician character below. There were at least two sizes of this coin, one that attains a weight of 7.79 g or larger, and the other 3.43 g or larger. A limited number of examples prevent us from being more precise than this regarding weight (see pl. 4 for our examples).

This combination of Tyche on the obverse and a date palm on the reverse was apparently abandoned for a time. When it appears again, it is on a series that runs from 26/5 B.C.E. to 14/5 C.E.[4] The reverse has been altered a bit. In the field about the trunk of the palm is the date and the monogram of the city with IEPAΣ below. Weights of the coins in this series range to 3.86 g or more (Hill 1965: 258-60; pl. 31: 11-13; see pl. 5 for our example). The next examples of this pair of motifs enters an era which we shall delay to discuss before examining another variation of coins with Tyche on the obverse.

The second major class of coins with Tyche on the obverse features a galley on the reverse side. The oldest of these, with dated specimens from the year 113/2 B.C.E. (LΔI, "year 14") is rather complicated. It pictures Astarte mounted in a galley that moves forward to our left. She holds something in her outstretched right hand; in her left is a cruciform standard. In left field is the Tyrian monogram; the date is to the right. Below, in Phoenician characters, we read *lṣr b*. The weights of the two specimens recorded in Hill are 3.52 and 2.65 g (1965: 254; pl. 31: 4).

The next series was struck for a great length of time—from 98/7 B.C.E. to 84/5 C.E. The iconography of the reverse features a galley moving left with the date, the monogram, and inscription above. As with the palm tree series that runs parallel to this series for 33 years, the inscription reads IE$^{A}$PA$\overset{\smallsmile}{\Sigma}$. Beneath is *lṣr* in Phoenician characters. The weights vie with those of the palm tree series, and one wonders why two coins of similar type and the same weight should have been struck at the same time. We can suggest that the two might not have been struck together in the same year, or that they represent the design privilege of different mint shops.

Running from 93/4 to 153/4 C.E. is a series of small coins that returns to the more complex pattern with which this class began, with Astarte standing in the galley. The inscriptional material is limited to the date, the monogram across the field above the ship, and *lṣr* in Phoenician characters below. A larger version of this coin appeared in 93/4 C.E. and was struck until 195/6 C.E. Like the palm tree and the Melqart coins that are contemporary to it, it bears the title *Metropolis* in the inscription, the full formula of which includes the date plus Ϸ ΙΕΡΑΣ/ΜΗΤΡΟΠΟ/ΛΕΩΣ/*lṣr*. The coins in this series weigh up to 9.32 g. This suggests three sizes of bronze coins for at least part of this period, for the two types described immediately below weigh up to 4.26 and 11.57 g respectively.

As we pointed out above, according to historical sources the title *Metropolis* was given to the city by Hadrian in response to a request put forth by Paulus of Tyre, but the precise date of this is difficult to determine. Hill asserts that some coins bear this title as early as 93/4 C.E., a date which precedes Hadrian and puts us into the period of Domitian (1965: cxxv). Our own material supports this early date, but whatever the exact time, it comes at the end of the 1st century C.E. and must be considered a matter of some importance to the city. The smallest coin of the series that follow this date is a type with Tyche on the obverse and the palm tree on the reverse. The series runs from 104/5 C.E. to 166/7 C.E. On the reverse we see the formula of the date across the field with the inscription written around from left upward to read ΜΗΤΡΟΠΟΛΕΩΣ ΙΕΡΑΣ (Hill 1965: 265-67; pl. 32: 2-3; see pl. 5 and note spelling and script of M77 1041).

The largest coin is a continuation of the series with Melqart on the obverse and the Tyrian war club and the monogram within an oak wreath on the reverse. The inscription is written around from upper right and reads simply ΜΗΤΡΟΠΟΛΕΩΣ (Hill 1965: 259-60; pl. 31: 14; see pls. 6-7 for our examples). These date from 93/4 to 136/7 C.E. and indicate, therefore, that the title was bestowed by Domitian rather than by Hadrian. A further elaboration of this type is seen in a series that runs parallel to this for almost the full extent of its period of currency. From 98/9 to 155/6 C.E. the Tyrians struck a coin with a reverse that features the club as above but with the inscription in horizontal lines as ΜΗ ΤΡΟ/ΠΟΛ ΕΩΣ/date *lṣr* (Hill 1965: 264-65; pl. 32: 1; see pls. 6-7 for our examples). It is hard to explain this, for there would seem to be no need for such a double series in that there are coins of both types in the same weight. It may well be, however—and Hill's examples plus our own limited supply bear this out—that the two types were not struck together in the same year. We have record of the first type for the years 93/4, 94/5, 115/6, 130/1, and 136/7 C.E. For the second type, we read dates of 98/9, 112/3, 152/3, and 155/6. Certainly we need more information before we can confirm this, but at the present it can be held as a plausible explanation.

To complicate the matter further, we know a series of coins in which the reverse inscription is expanded to ΤΥΡΟΥ/ΜΗ ΤΡΟ/ΕΩΣ/date *lṣr*, with

TYPOY replacing the monogram at the top of the Heraklean club. This series extends from 112/3 to 183/4 C.E. (Hill 1965: 267; pl. 32: 4; see pl. 8 for our example). Again, the weights approximate the weights of the coins above. One can only suspect that competing shops were authorized to produce coins in different years and that the dates represent the time of the authorization rather than the year in which each particular coin was actually struck.

The last in the series of coins with Melqart on the obverse features the temple of the Koinon with its eight columns, a podium of two steps and some object on the pediment. Around, from left upward, is an inscription that reads KOINOY ΦΟΙΝΙΚΗC. Beneath, in the exergue, are the letters AKT, or at times, AKTI (Hill 1965: 268; pl. 132: 5-6; see pls. 8-9 for our examples). If we take AKT to be a date, it brings us to 195/6 C.E. It seems strange, however, that every known specimen of this type should have the same date. Moreover, the occurrence of AKTI defies this interpretation. Perhaps the formula has something to do with the founding of the Koinon or the completion of a new basilica in which the governing council of plutarchs met to transact city business and see to such matters as the issuing of coins. The AKT could represent the date of such an event. The I could abbreviate some term relative to the founding.[5]

The autonomous coinage ended then, with only two types enduring to that point: the small coin with Tyche on the obverse and the galley on the reverse and, as just mentioned, the large Melqart bronze with the Koinon on the reverse.[6] At this point in time the coinage was taken over by the Roman emperors and coins in their honor began to appear at the Tyrian mint in 201 C.E. or shortly thereafter. That is when Septimius Severus declared the site his colony.

## NOTES

[1]We find the same motif on Jewish coins of the Persian period; thus, there must have been a general tendency to copy Attic money. The owl on the Jewish coins has no flail or crook, of course, and on some examples one sees a lily to the left and on others, a small rosette beneath the lily (Meshorer 1967: pl. 1).

[2]Examples of all the types described above can be seen in the plates at the end of Newell (1923). See Newell (1923: 16-21) for a summary of dating this and the other series of its kind. The scheme he finally suggested was as follows:

| In the year | 307 | B.C. |
|---|---|---|
| " | 306 | B.C. |
| " | 305 | B.C. |
| " | 304 | B.C. |
| " | 303 | B.C. |
| " | 302 | B.C. |
| " | 301 | B.C. |
| and so forth to the year | 287 | B.C. |

[3]Melqart/Herakles was very much the city's god. Even in Carthage they felt reverence for Tyrian Herakles. During Seleucid times there was a festival to Herakles every five years that must have

been more of a blending of Tyrian and Greek ideas than a Greek innovation only. See Jidejian 1969: 70, 95, and 105 where the author asserts that Herakles had become an eternal-life figure, a savior promising what all saviors promised.

[4]Hill says 18/7 B.C.E., but we have one clear coin of this type with simply P (100) as a date. See GH 77 1275 below.

[5]We are aware of the fact that Roman coins are typically commemorative in nature, that is to say that the Romans used coins to announce an important event such as the accession or promotion of an emperor, the conquest of a territory, or a public oath of loyalty on the part of the emperor. I believe that this function of coins also prevailed in the provinces and the cities. The erection of a public building would be an event worthy of commemoration. Perhaps many of the coins that picture a building were struck to announce the completion or renovation of the structure, and if this is the case, the coin under discussion here is a clue to the date of the erection of the building and pictures the KOINON ΦOINIKHC. In 3rd-century coinage of Tyre we shall see coins that similarly commemorate the staging of the Heraklean games at various intervals. Perhaps at earlier times a coin with the bust of Herakles/Melqart was struck anew at each staging of the games. This might unlock the mystery of the unaccountable gaps in the dates that are registered on those coins.

[6]H. Hamburger (1954: 208) maintains that autonomous coinage of the smaller types continues "late into the 3rd century A.D." The example he gives on p. 208 bears the letters ANT above IЕ̂P AΣ̌, and he reads that as the date 351, which calculates to 235/6 C.E.

# CHAPTER 3
# THE TYRIAN CITY COINS OF THE 3RD CENTURY C.E.

The Tyrian city coins of the 3rd century occur in such a variety of types that they deserve some commentary. Surely, their many motifs reveal something of the culture of the city during that time and something of how the Hellenistic and Roman influences of the times merged or had merged with native influences. Tyre may have been exceptional, of course, but its case would still serve as an interesting study. More likely—and the evidence I have scanned makes it seem so—something of what was happening at this one city of the Levant was happening at other important cities of that area in that time. In pondering what was going on at Tyre we may gain some depth of understanding of the general situation of the Roman Empire in the East. As a matter of procedure I shall begin by describing the coins that were struck under each succeeding emperor and empress, noting the introduction of new types when they occur in order to emphasize the iconography of the coins above all else. It is in that iconography that I think I can discover most of what I have in mind.

The first coins in these series are those of Septimius Severus (193-211 C.E.), who elevated the city to the status of Colony. It was this declaration that inaugurated this entire group of coins we are about to examine. We do not know the exact year in which these first examples were struck, for they are all undated. We know of a single type: a coin that honors the founding of the colony and, at once, the presence of the Third or Gallic Legion. The portrait and title of the emperor are on the obverse. The legend reads LSEPT-SEVRERTAVGIMPXI. The reverse of the coin pictures a founder plowing with a team of ox and cow. He is veiled, and that leads us to suspect that he is a deified character. In the background is the top of a standard surmounted by a leaf and inscribed with LEG III GAL. Around is the inscribed formula that will appear in some version on all coins except most of those of Elagabalus: SEPTVRVSMETROP with COLONI in the exergue below (Hill 1965: 269). The title indicates the dual pride of the city as a municipality of the Roman Empire and as a Colony of Septimius.

Struck in honor of Julia Domna Augusta (193-211) during the reign of Septimius Severus was a coin that featured some of the sacred symbols of the city of Tyre. The central feature on the reverse of one type is Astarte wearing a turreted crown on her head, a chiton and a himation on her body as she stands with her foot on the prow of a galley. She holds a sceptre and is being crowned by Nike, who stands on a column at our right. To the left is a small figure of "Marsyas of the Forum" carrying a wineskin. Above it is a trophy which Astarte touches with her right hand. At the bottom of the coin, just to the right of the goddess from our perspective, is the Tyrian murex shell (Hill 1965: 269; pl. 32: 7). The blending of Roman with traditional motifs in this scene was likely meant to say something to the effect that Rome is now granting a blessing to the venerable city. Specifically, it is the Victory-gift that makes Astarte the accepted guardian-queen of the site. The little figure with the wineskin, the prow of the galley, and the murex shell all promise prosperity in terms familiar to the history of Tyre. The message is the political gospel of Rome.

As we shall see, this coin design will persist to the end. It was struck under Caracalla, Elagabalus, Severus Alexander, Gordian III, Phillip Sr., Trebonianus Gallus, Volusianus, Valerianus, and Gallienus. It endured for 65 years with only slight variations in the design.

Less specifically Tyrian in its iconography is a coin with a togated, veiled male figure holding a sceptre as he sacrifices at an altar. At the man's feet is a murex shell (Hill 1965: 270; pl. 32: 8). Who is the man? It would seem to be the emperor. The other possibility is that it might be the priest of Sol Invictus, Elagabalus. Since Septimius Severus was a supporter of the cult and of the priestly house of Emesa, during this period one must watch for signs of the introduction and increasing importance of this religious movement (Halsberghe 1972: 49-51).

A third type of Tyrian coin struck for Julia Domna pictures a bull walking to the right with the standard of the Third Legion behind. To the right, beneath the bull's head, is the murex shell (Hill 1965: 270; pl. 33: 9). The figure of the bull, though not specifically Tyrian, was familiar to the religious history of the Phoenicians. At the same time, however, or just as likely, it served as symbol for the Third Legion that is honored by the coin. Did they pick up the mascot locally or did they bear it with them from distant points? Both are equally possible. We shall see this motif continued in the reigns of Caracalla, Macrinus, and Trebonianus Gallus.

On the fourth Tyrian coin of Julia known to myself, one sees nude Melqart/Herakles standing toward the left, holding in his left hand the club and lion skin. Above his outstretched right hand are a pair of cylindrical objects that in earlier iconography would pass as phallic symbols but may simply be labeled *baetyls* here. (The word is a corruption of beth-el, "god-house.") Beneath the arm is an incense altar, and to our right, between the altar and the standing figure, is the murex shell (Jidejian 1969: no. 88 in the plates). The twin baetyls will become an increasingly common motif on these coins. This precise design was also used by Gordian III.

The reverse inscription on all four of these coins is the same: SEP TVRVS METRO COLON. On the obverse the legend simply reads IVLIA AVGVSTA. H. Hamburger (1954: 206, 220) reports a coin of Julia Domna with an eagle on the reverse, wreath in beak, and perched on a palm branch. The inscription around begins with SEP. . . .

The bearded countenance of Caracalla (196-211/17) is always stern and frowning. The burdens of the empire must have hung heavily upon him from the beginning. By expression alone one would take him to be a ruthless man. Eldest son of Severus and Julia Domna, he was given the rank of Caesar Augustus while yet a child. When his aging father died at York in 211, he became sole emperor under the title and name that appears as the legend on the obverses of his coins: IMP MA AVR ANTONINVS. The reverses of his Tyrian coins are all struck with the combination, SEP TVRVS METRO COLONI.

There were ten distinct reverse types struck at Tyre under his regime. Three of these types already have been listed above as coins of Julia Domna: (1) the Astarte scene as on the first reverse described above, (2) the togated male figure performing a sacrifice as on the second reverse described above, and (3) the bull walking to the right with the standard of the Third Legion behind as on the third reverse of Julia Domna's coins. The other seven types follow.

Unique to Caracalla, as far as I know, is a reverse that pictures the Greco-Egyptian Harpocrates ("Horus-the-infant") with a himation around the lower part of his body and draped over his left arm. On his head is the appropriate lotus flower. His right hand is to his lips as though he were sucking his thumb, and he bears a cornucopia in his left arm. Below we see a lighted altar at our left and a murex shell at our right (Hill 1965: 270; pl. 33: 10).

Another coin displays Nike facing us in a semistanding position as she leans on a column to her left. She holds a wreath in her right hand, a palm branch in her left. Midway up in left field is the murex shell (Hill 1965: 271; pl. 32: 11). The total scene, with its blending of Greco-Roman and Tyrian motifs, speaks the same message as the first coin of Julia Domna above—victory and prosperity for Tyre—except that here the Tyrian motifs are clearly subordinate.

A sixth coin type of Caracalla features the temple of the Phoenician Koinon as seen from the perspective of a view from the right front corner. It has five columns in the front, eight at the side. In the exergue we see the murex shell between two palm branches (Hill 1965: 271; pl. 32: 12). This is Tyrian, and with this we must suggest that the Koinon was at this time the house of governors, wealthy citizens perhaps, who met to discuss the commercial and political affairs of the city. Such an oligarchy was by no means new to the Phoenician cities, of course. From ancient times they had been ruled by a small group of wealthy elders. The adoption of the Greek institution of the Koinon was not a radical innovation for these people. Presumably, this was the institution that supervised the striking of the city coins.

In commemoration of the Heraklean games that were held in Tyre, one coin type pictures an agonistic table supporting two prize crowns. Complementing this Hellenistic theme are a palm branch on either side and a murex shell below (Hill 1965: 271; pl. 32: 13).[1] Above we read ACTIA; below, ERACLIA.

A second coin commemorating the games pictures a prize crown with ACTIA inscribed across and a palm tree above it (Jidejian 1969: no. 91 in the plates).

A ninth coin reverse features a draped figure standing before an altar at our left. I cannot identify this figure other than to suggest that it is either the emperor or a priest.[2] This coin design was repeated by Gordian III.

Among our discoveries at Meiron was a coin of Caracalla with a reverse that features a figure standing with both arms down. Behind, at right, is Victory on a pedestal extending a wreath. All other details are worn away. A similar coin is pictured in Hill 1965: pl. 32: 7, but it is not identical to the one that we have found (pl. 1C: M71 1573).

Geta, the younger brother of Caracalla who was murdered by that same brother in 212 C.E., had a countenance much like that of his father. His title on the legends of the Tyrian coins struck in his honor appears as IMP GETA CAESAR. There is only one reverse type. It features an eagle with the body facing and wings outspread but the head turned to our left. In the background is the standard of the Gallian Legion III. SEP TVRVS METROP is inscribed around, COLONI in the exergue (Hill 1965: 272). One wonders why the eagle was used to represent the Third Legion here while a bull is used on other coins of the same period. Jidejian (1969: 104) reminds us that the eagle was the symbol of the god of the sky. Could this be a token of the introduction of the sun cult? A variant of this design was issued by Gallienus in a later decade.

Macrinus, one of the conspirators who murdered Caracalla, ruled only 14 months before being captured and put to death by the forces of Julia Maesa and her grandson, Bassanius, who is more commonly known as Elagabalus. As short as was his time of tenure, however, we know of at least three coin types struck in his honor at Tyre. The obverse legend on all three reads IMP CAES MACRINVS AVG.

On the reverse of one coin we see the Phoenician Koinon from the right-front-quarter perspective, much as on a coin of Caracalla above but with a star in the pediment. The inscription around reads COENV PHOENICES. In the exergue we find N plus another letter—in the specimens recorded by Hill, either A or I (1965: 272; pl. 32: 14, 15). If these are dates in Greek numerals, they read 70 plus the value of the second letter. But this is unlikely in that the I has the value of 10 and 80 (70 plus 10) and would hardly be written as NI when it could have been done more simply as O. Perhaps the N stands for the Latin *numero* and the character A or I for the number of a mint shop. There are further examples of this phenomenon.

A second coin type pictures the bull walking rightward as on the third coin of Julia Domna examined above. As on that other coin, we see the standard of LEG III GAL in the background (Hill 1965: 272).

A third coin type pictures a galley with oars and rudder. There is a murex shell above and the usual inscription in the circumference and exergue, as with the other two types done for Macrinus (Hill 1965: 272).

The predominance of native Tyrian motifs on the coins of Macrinus might indicate that he was bidding strongly for the support of this city. A cursory examination of the coins of Tripoli and, to a lesser degree, Berytus and Byblos, leads one to think that he used the same technique there (Hill 1965: 102, 221). In his position, having done what he did, he probably needed all the help he could get.

Diadumenian (218 C.E.), the son of Macrinus, was executed soon after his father. On the Tyrian coins struck for him during his brief time we read the title MOP DIADVMENIANVS CAES. Two types of reverses are seen, both as thoroughly Tyrian in iconography as those of his father. One depicts a scene with Astarte in the center as on the first coin of Julia Domna we examined or the first coin of Caracalla. A second coin features a simple palm tree with CO LO/NI across the field and SEP TVRVS METRP around (Hill 1965: 273; pl. 32: 17).

Bassanius (218-22), more commonly known as Elagabalus, was a central figure in the movement that eventually led to the establishment of the sun-god cult of Emesa as the official religion of the emperors. It is beyond the province of this cursory sketch to examine the details of this movement, but it is important to note that this emperor functioned more as high priest of the sun cult than as effective emperor. The power was apparently in the hands of his grandmother, Julia Maesa, and, to a lesser extent, his mother, Julia Soaemias. The emperor himself was a 14-year-old boy when he acceded to the throne, and from the beginning he served as priest of Sol Invictus Elagabalus (hence his priestly name) rather than as political head of the empire. Indeed, he quite soon had himself castrated so as to serve in his priestly role with purer dedication. For all of this it is wise to think that the coins struck for him might just as well be termed coins of Julia Maesa (see Halsberghe 1972: 57-60).

In view of the emperor's strong personal interest in the cult of the sun-god of Emesa, one could expect attention to that in the iconography of his coins. We do find such coins from Emesa, of course,[3] but at Tyre the symbols cater to the local or to broadly syncretistic taste, as we see in the following examples.

On the obverses of these coins, the emperor is wearing the paladumentum and armor characteristic of the period. His bust is remarkably youthful and handsome. He is portrayed as the idol of the army more than as high priest of the Sun. His title, likewise, satisfied political rather than religious demands, for it reads, as Caracalla's, IMP CAES MAV ANTONINVS AVG. Reverse types include the following:

Astarte, being crowned as in the first coin of Julia Domna we examined, is continued for Elagabalus as it was for Caracalla and Diadumenian. Apparently, this combination of motifs was appreciated particularly by the oligarchic council of Tyre. To make it even more thoroughly Tyrian, the version of this coin done for Elagabalus adds a palm tree on the left and a murex shell on the right (Hill 1965: 273; pl. 33: 1).

On a second coin type we see the temple of Astarte from a frontal view with its six columns and arched entrance. A pellet is seen on the space above the arch. Does it depict a star or a planet? Astarte fills the space beneath the arch, in company with the victory at our right and the trophy at our left, creating a miniature version of the scene depicted in the coin immediately preceding (Hill 1965: 276; pl. 33: 3). Surely this must be a scene depicting the temple as it stood in the city and the actual statuary that must have been there. It must have been one of the most sacred features of the city, and one to which the emperors felt obliged to pay tribute for the entire period in which the colonial coins were struck.[4] SEPTIM TVR COL is inscribed around.

On a third coin type we see two oxen or bulls walking to the right. Behind is the inscribed standard of LEG III GAL. The murex shell appears in the right field. SEPTIM TVRO is inscribed around, COLO in the exergue (Hill 1965: 274). This continues the basic motif of the coin, with the single bull and the standard behind that we noted above. It is a coin honoring the Roman legion that was stationed at Tyre.

At a point early in his reign, Elagabalus deprived the city of its status as Metropolis and Colony. From this point on the coins of Elagabalus have only

the word TVRIORVM inscribed on the reverse, a decision which may have
been made by Julia Maesa, who likely had difficulties in getting parts of the
empire to recognize the authority of her grandson. Hill suggests that the city
had probably supported Macrinus against Elagabalus (1965: cxxv-cxxvi).

First in the TVRIORVM series is the complete Astarte scene described
above, including the palm tree and the murex shell. One variant places the
murex shell in the exergue rather than in the field (Hill 1965: 275; pl. 33: 2). The
temple of Astarte, with this scene beneath the arch, is also found in this series
(Hill 1965: 276; pl. 33: 3).

A distinctive type, not to be repeated, pictures a nude Dionysos standing
and facing us in the prow of a galley, with his head turned to our left. In his left
hand he holds the Bacchic wand, in his right hand the kantharos or scarab
beetle. A seated panther looks up at him. In front left we see two bound
captives seated by a trophy. The murex shell is in right field; a star is above (Hill
1965: 276). This is a curious mixture of symbols. The captives and trophy
should signal some kind of military victory, but the figure of Dionysos hardly
fits such a theme.

Following the theme of the third coin of Caracalla we saw above, we see
Nike, who carries no wreath, but in whose left hand is the palm branch. In place
of the wreath is a murex shell, which seems a striking tribute to the colony.
A palm tree stands to our left (Hill 1965: 276; pl. 33: 4).

Fourth in our sequence of TVRIORVM coins is a nude male figure
running to the right with four stags running behind in the same direction. He
has a chlamys draped over his left arm; there is a star above, a murex shell
below, and an uncertain object to the right (Hill 1965: 277; pl. 33: 5). The
identity of the character is not clear, but according to a recent study of this coin
done by Ernst Will (1973: 80-84), it is Herakles/Usoos as founder of Tyre.
Apart from that one could suspect that it is a depiction of the sun-god. In early
mythology it is Enkidu, the wild companion of Gilgamesh, who races
with stags.

Illustrating one of the prouder moments in Tyre's history with a tale made
famous among Romans by Virgil is a coin that depicts Dido building Carthage
—and lest there be any doubt about her identity, the exergue contains the
inscription ΔΕΙΔΩΝ. The goddess carries a ruler and a sceptre. A mason works
on one of the towers above the arched gateway to the city while a man below
digs with a pick. The murex shell is above, a palm tree to our right (Hill 1965:
277; pl. 33: 6). Though Tyre had been demoted in status by Elagabalus and
Julia Maesa, the designers were free to assert Tyrian pride.

Continuing this theme is a coin that depicts Dido in a galley, holding a
cornucopia in her left hand, a short sceptre in her right. Forward in the ship is a
sailor, while a helmsman bends over the rudder at the stern that is ornamented
with a shield or an aphlaston. In the exergue are two murex shells (Hill 1965:
277). As far as I know, this coin was not repeated.

Picking up a popular Greek tale of the accomplishments of Tyre in its
history, another coin depicts Kadmos, the legendary bringer of the alphabet
from Phoenicia to Greece, in a galley. His right hand is extended as though
proffering his gift. In left field is the murex shell (Hill 1965: 277).[5] Such themes

as this make one suspect that the Tyrians were doing their best to demonstrate to the emperor that they deserved the status they had once been given but which had been taken away.

Eighth in the series of TVRIORVM coins is a reverse that pictures a quadriga advancing toward our left, with the nearest horse looking back. In the car a male figure stands holding a sceptre in his left hand while his right is raised high. Above the horses we see a star, as the star above the stags in the fourth coin of this TVRIORVM series. In the exergue is a murex shell and a palm branch (Hill 1965: 278; pl. 33: 7). One must surmise that here we have a depiction of the sun-god proclaimed as Sol Invictus Heligabal at Emesa. The sun-chariot and the day-star in combination can only depict the rising of Helios, who was destined to assume an official position in the religion of the empire. While the ancient symbols of Tyre persist and the populace is reminded of the proud history of the grand old city, the ruling power was promoting the new religion of the sun in symbols that could be understood from more than one source.

A ninth coin with TVRIORVM on the reverse depicts an ovoid baetyl encircled by a serpent (Hill 1965: 278; pl. 33: 8). One wonders if this was the sacred sun-stone that.was venerated at Emesa, but sources indicate that that was a conical stone (the coins referred to in n. 3, above, give us this depiction).

Commemorating the games is a coin with a prize crown on the reverse, inscribed with HPAKLIA O VM . . . KAIC . . . (an incomplete inscription due to wear). A palm branch projects from the upper opening. TVRIORVM is written around in the circumference; below is a murex shell and B (Hill 1965: 278).

To the author's mild surprise, the coins of Elagabalus do not betray very much of the campaign to promote the worship of Sol Invictus. To the contrary, they do more to elevate the status of Tyre. This causes one to wonder who had the most direct control over the design of the coins. If it was the emperor, one would expect more evidence of the growing sun cult. Yet one gains the impression that Tyre was a stronghold of old religions that would no more give way to Sol Invictus than to Christianity. That it could tolerate competing religious ideas was clear enough. It was the claim to dominance or exclusiveness that Tyrians apparently resisted (Halsberghe 1972: 76-78). The emphasis on the legendary history of Tyre suggests that local leaders were trying to convince the imperial government that Tyre was deserving of the honor that had been taken from it early in the reign of Bassanius. One suspects that the council of those who met at the Koinon had considerable authority and freedom in designing at least some of the city coins. They obviously had to depict the emperor or the empress, with the correct and complete title of that person, on the obverse of each coin, but in the iconography of the reverse there may have been some freedom. Only the inscription of the reverse seems to have been rigidly controlled. Or were these various designs on the reverses the rulers' attempt to gain support from the city? Either way, the feelings of the local leaders were being respected.

Aquilia Severa, the bride of Elagabalus in 220 C.E., was honored by at least three coin reverses. She had been one of the Vestal Virgins before her marriage to the emperor-priest. Her bust is draped, and she wears a crescent in her hair. Her title is inscribed as IVL AQVILIA SEVERA AVG. The attribution to Tyre on the reverses is, as with all but the first coins of Elagabalus, simply TVRIORVM.

As described above, one type bears the motif of Astarte being crowned by Nike. A second type, like another of the coins of Elagabalus, pictures Nike carrying a wreath and a palm branch. A third, also like one of the coins of Elagabalus, features a prize crown with a palm tree emerging from its middle. Inscribed on it we read HPAKΛIA OΛV/MΠKAA../.ΛI.[6] The murex shell and B are below (Hill 1965: 279; pl. 33: 11). The presence of the B is intriguing. It must stand for the same as whatever the *bet* stood for on an earlier series of coins. No suggestions worthy of arguing come to mind. Perhaps it is for Baal.

Severus Alexander (222-35 C.E.) was engineered into office as Caesar in 221 in order to become emperor when Elagabalus was removed. Only a youth of fourteen at the death of his cousin-turned-stepfather, he remained under the influence of his mother, Julia Mammaea. He appears bareheaded, in paladumentum and armor, and his image is youthful enough to be confused with that of Elagabalus on his earliest coins were it not for his titles, which read M AV ALEXANDER CAES SE and IMP CAES(MAVRSEV) ALEX-ANDER AVG.

On the reverses of his Tyrian coins two familiar motifs are continued: Astarte being crowned by Nike and the temple of the Phoenician Koinon from right-front-quarter perspective. We know that Tyre had been restored to colonial status from the inscription around on those obverses which read SEP TVRO MET(RO) COL (Hill 1965: 279-80).

Since I know of no sure examples of coins for Maximinus among those struck at Tyre, we must say that there may have been a gap from the year 235 to 238 when no coins were struck. This seems unlikely, of course. One would expect that someday an example or some examples will be found. Adhering to what is known to date, however, we must move to the coins of Gordian III (238-44 C.E.), who was proclaimed Augustus by the Praetorian guards. After suppressing revolts in Africa, he directed campaigns against Persia until he was deposed and murdered by his own troops. His laureate bust, with paladumentum and armor, is surrounded by the title IMP GORDIANVS PIVS FEL AVG. The regular reverse inscription for the coins of Gordian III is COL TVR METR.

Most of the reverses struck in his honor continue established types: (1) the scene of Astarte being crowned by Tyche, (2) the frontal view of the temple of Astarte, (3) Melqart/Herakles with club and lion skin pouring a libation over a burning altar, (4) the male figure that we suggested might be Sol Invictus of Emesa (fourth in the TVRIORVM sequence above). Two coin designs introduce Kadmos, the legendary person who carried the Phoenician alphabet to Greece. In both, Kadmos is nude and holds a club in his left hand. In one of these two types, with his right hand he hurls a stone at a serpent that has reared up against him. In the other, Kadmos merely stands facing our left with a palm tree behind and a murex shell to our left (Hill 1965: 280-81; pl. 33: 12-13; Jidejian 1969: no. 93 in the plates).

On a coin found at Meiron we see a seminude goddess—Nike perhaps—extending her right arm over a palm tree at left, with a murex shell at right and what appears to be a bird beneath. Between the palm tree and the goddess appears the letter N. Above the murex shell, the letter I (see p. 65 and pl. 14: M74 097). Hamburger (1954: 224) reports a coin featuring Dido in a galley as in Hill (1965: pl. 44: 9). She holds a cornucopia in her left hand and a short sceptre in her right hand. Forward is a sailor moving right. At the stern is a helmsman bending over his rudder. In the field is the Phoenician inscription, ʾlt ṣr. There is a murex shell below the ship. The inscription around reads C OLTVRME.

The ambrosial rocks—two "baetyls" or rock cones—appear on three of the coins of Gordian III. On the Melqart/Herakles coin mentioned above we see them in miniature above and to the left; water escapes from beneath them. In two other reverse designs they are the prominent central motif. On one, they rest on a single base, and we see a crescent and a star between. In the exergue is inscribed AMBPOCIE AITPE, accompanied by a murex shell between two palm branches. On the other design, each stone has a separate base, and there is an olive tree between them (Hill 1965: 281; pl. 33: 14-15). It is from Philo of Byblos that we learn that Tyre was originally an island of two floating rocks called the "ambrosial rocks." On one of the peaks grew an olive tree of Astarte sheltered by a curtain of flame. There was an eagle perched on top of the tree to watch over a serpent that coiled around its trunk. According to the legend, the island would cease to float when someone would succeed in sacrificing the eagle to the gods. Usoos/Herakles taught the people how to make boats. Then he set off for the island, and the eagle offered itself voluntarily for sacrifice. As soon as its blood was shed, Tyre rooted itself (see Jidejian 1969 for a summary of sources and bibliographical details). The coin motifs that suggest this story are highly religious and political. In combination, they are a promise of life to the city and its inhabitants, perhaps even the eternal life that was so commonly offered by the mysteries of the time. In conjunction with this, we must recall that Christianity was rising in strength at this time, both at Tyre and throughout the empire. It is interesting that the authorities of Tyre preferred these Hellenistic-Oriental motifs to the Christian symbols or ideas. The twin rocks will appear frequently on coin designs from this point onward.

Philip Senior (242-49 C.E.) reigned during the 1000th anniversary of the founding of Rome which occurred in 248 C.E. Magnificent games were staged for the occasion. Though there were imperial coins to commemorate this celebration (ROMAE AETERNAE and others), we see little hint of it in the coins of Tyre. His own legend reads IMP IVL PHILIPPVS P F AVG. The inscription on the reverses of these coins reads COL TVRO METRO. Two coin reverses continue familiar motifs in honor of the traditional fertility goddess of the Levant, the one that displays Astarte being crowned by Nike and the reverse type that shows a frontal view of the Astarte temple. Astarte is also honored in one of the new designs introduced under Philip, a scene that depicts a sacrifice to Astarte similar to the first coin above but with four figures of cities wearing turreted crowns filling the lower half of the coin. The Tyche to the left stands with right hand upraised; the second holds a dish of offerings; the third pours a libation on an altar; the fourth is in the position of the first (Hill 1965: 282; pl. 34: 1). Who are these four city goddesses? Tyre, Ptolemais-Ace, and Berytus were striking coins at the time. It is hard to imagine any city other than Sidon for the fourth. But this assumes that they are all Phoenician cities. Perhaps they are meant to depict four great Roman cities of the east. If so, Antioch and Alexandria must be two candidates. This coin was repeated by Trebonianus Gallus.

Kadmos emerges again on a coin that depicts him in company with the Roman goddess Harmonia. He stands nude, at the left, with a chlamys over his left shoulder and a spear in his left hand. The right hands of both characters are clasped. Harmonia is draped in a long chiton and a himation. She holds what appears to be an architect's square in her left hand. Behind her we see the front of a heifer; between the two figures is a murex shell (Hill 1965: 283; pl. 34: 2). The whole scene is strikingly syncretistic and with the obvious political intent of announcing good times and even a building program for Tyre based on peaceful cooperation with Roman authority.

On the reverse of a third coin that was introduced by Philip, we see a shrine from quarter perspective. It has a flat roof supported by two pillars. The base rests on four short legs; carrying poles project from it. Within the shrine is a smaller one containing an ovoid baetyl with a flat cap between two figures (Hill 1965: 283). Is this the sun-stone of Emesa? This coin was repeated by Valerian.

Hamburger (1954: 226) reports a bronze tetradrachma of Otacilia Severa, wife of Philip Senior, with Kadmos moving right in a galley as in Hill (1965: pl. 44: 11). This is a larger and more complete scene than that of the same motif first struck for Elagabalus (Hill 1965: pl. 34: 17). Among the details is a murex shell and an aphlaston.

One Tyrian coin of Decius Trajan (249-51 C.E.) came to light in our 1972 excavations at Meiron. The bust on the obverse is crowned with a radiate crown. The inscription around is incomplete but clearly reads . . . TRAIANVSAVG. On the reverse is nude Diomede standing to the left with his right foot on a rock, his left arm resting on a spear. A chlamys hangs over his left arm. His right hand holds a palladium; beneath it, in left field, is the murex shell. The inscription around reads COLTV RO MET (see p. 66 and pl. 14: M72 2282).

We have a series of coins for Trebonianus Gallus (251-53 C.E.). The bust is in the appearance of all emperors in this series up to the example of Decius Trajan, that is, facing right with laureate crown and wearing paladumentum and armor. The legend around reads IMP C BVBIVS TREBO GALLVS AVG. There are nine types of reverses to date. The first four are repetitions of coins previously struck. One continues the series of coins depicting Astarte being crowned by Nike. A second repeats the scene of Astarte with the four city goddesses below. A third repeats the coin depicting Dido as builder of Carthage (inscribed in the exergue: ΔIΔW). A fourth is the coin honoring LEG III GAL with the patron bull (Hill 1965: 283-85).

Fig. 5. The dog finding the murex shell on the beach as seen on a coin of the mid-3rd century C.E. Drawn by Carol Adamac.

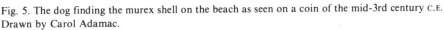

One of the new coins pictures a portable shrine with an arched roof on two columns; two carrying poles project from beneath. Inside is a bust of veiled Astarte with a turreted crown—or so says Hill (1965: 283). But if this is Astarte, she has had her identity merged with that of Tyche, the city's "fortuna." Astarte has not appeared in this crown before. The murex shell is in the exergue beneath (Hill 1965: 283; pl. 34: 3). I, for one, am not surprised by this apparent merging of the Phoenician Astarte and the Greek Tyche. I suspect that the merging was already present long before this and that the Tyche in turreted bust on the coins of the autonomous era was already a representation of the city's Astarte. This particular coin will be repeated by Gallienus.

A second new coin design pictures Herakles and Apollo as Gemini. Both are nude and in frontal position with arms on each other's shoulders and looking at each other. Herakles holds his club, Apollo his lyre. There is a murex shell between (Hill 1965: 284; pl. 34: 4). The coin is not repeated as far as I know.

The twin baetyls appear in a scene with an olive tree between and, to the right, a dog finding a murex shell on the beach (Hill 1965: 284; fig. 5 in our text). The dog finding a murex shell goes back to a legend recounted by Achilles Tatius (Jidejian 1969: 118), an old tale told by the Tyrians that a shepherd's dog bit into a murex after it had been tossed aside by a fisherman. As the man attempted to wash the dog's mouth because of the purple stain that covered it, his own hands became stained with the juice of the murex. He poured some of the fluid on sheep's wool and thus discovered the dye for which the Phoenicians became famous. This coin was repeated by Valerian.

The Heraklean games were commemorated by a fourth new coin that displays two prize crowns with AKT incised into one and HPA into the other. Between but above the crowns, we see two old motifs of a club hung downward and two palm branches. The murex shell is below (Hill 1965: 285; pl. 34: 6).

In 1971 we found a coin of Trebonianus Gallus at Khirbet Shema$^c$, with a laureate bust and the legend [IMPCG]VIB[IVSTREBO]GALL[VSAVG]. On the reverse are three figures in a galley, the central figure towering taller than the others. The larger figure is male and nude from the waist upward. At least one of the small figures may be a child. I am hesitant to try to identify any (see p. 00 and pl. 14: KS71 1310). The reverse inscription for all of the reverses of Decius Trajan and Trebonianus Gallus is COL TVRO METRO.

Volusianus, son of Trebonianus Gallus, was also his contemporary as coruler. Father and son were murdered together in Italy by their own troops. The legend on the obverse of the son's coins reads IMP C G VIB VOLVSIANVS AVG. On one of his coins we see the temple of Astarte with its six columns. Another coin repeats the scene of Dido building Carthage, with ΔIΔWN inscribed below (Hill 1965: 285-86).

Two new coin types were introduced. One features Kadmos, nude and running to the right, on a galley. He carries a sword in his left hand and beckons with his right as he looks back at followers whom we must imagine. In the exergue is the murex shell (Hill 1965: 286). This coin persists through the reigns of Valerian and Gallienus. A second new coin portrays Hermes/Thoth, standing nude to the waist. He holds a rolled papyrus in his right hand, a caduceus in his left. At his feet, to the left, is an ibis; at the right we see a palm tree with a murex shell above (Hill 1965: 286). The coin reappears under Valerian and Salonina. The mix of Greek, Egyptian, and Phoenician motifs well represents the syncretism of the times. The reverse inscription on these coins reads COL TVRO METRO.

Valerian Senior (253-60 C.E.), who ended his career as a prisoner of the Persians, left us a large variety of coins as his legacy at Tyre. The legend on the obverses reads IMP C P LIC VALERIANVS AVG. The reverse inscription on these coins reads COL TVRO MET. The bust shows him in paladumentum and armor, either laureate or wearing a radiate crown. Several of his coins are a continuation of prior designs: (1) the scene of Astarte crowned by Nike, (2) a frontal view of the temple of Astarte, (3) Hermes/Thoth carrying the papyrus roll and the caduceus, (4) Nike standing with a wreath in her right hand and a palm branch in her left, (5) Kadmos running on a galley as he beckons to followers, (6) Dido building Carthage, (7) the shrine with flat roof and an ovoid baetyl inside, (8) an olive tree between the "ambrosial rocks" (Hill 1965: 286-91).

Several new designs also emerge. On one we see Roma (or Athena), sitting on what could be either a sphere or a low-backed chair. She wears a helmet, a chiton and himation and holds in her right hand a pair of statuettes on a prow. With her left she leans on a spear, and there is a shield below that. The murex shell is in the exergue (Hill 1965: 287). This coin is repeated by Gallienus.

Another coin that will be repeated by Gallienus features nude Melqart/ Herakles standing as he holds his club and lion skin in his left hand. His right hand rests on a trophy; there is a murex shell in the left field (Hill 1965: 288).

A third new type pictures Okeanos reclining to the left, draped from the waist down and wearing crabs' claws on his head. In his left hand he holds an oar while he stretches his right to the "ambrosial rocks" from which water is flowing. The name WKEANOC is actually inscribed in the exergue. The murex shell is in left field (Hill 1965: 289). The scene at once pays tribute to the founding of Tyre and, in the religious language of the time, suggests that there was new life for the old sea-god in the waters of the sacred stones. The theme of reviving old religious forces was common, as we have noted, and Tyre gives us examples of specific instances of that phenomenon through its coins. This coin was repeated for Salonina.

A fourth new coin reverse depicts a river-god, beardless, with a wreath on his head, dressed in himation from waist downward. In his left hand he holds a reed with long leaves; his right hand is pointing toward something. The murex shell is in the field right, and there is a small half-figure of a river-god below (Hill 1965: 289; pl. 34: 11). We found a coin of this type at Khirbet Shemaᶜ in 1972. On our specimen, the object to which the river-god is pointing seems to be a plant growing out of a rock (see p. 66 and pl. 15: M75 436).

A fifth new type shows Europa, dressed in a long chiton and himation and holding a vase in her left hand as she holds her right hand over her breast. A bull, coming out of water, approaches her from the left. Above we see the ambrosial rocks with an olive tree between, below, a murex shell (Hill 1965: 290; pl. 34: 14).

One type appeared first as a coin of Decius Trajan in our archeological records (see above). It is the coin that depicts nude Diomede standing to left with his right foot on a rock, his left arm resting on a spear. Because Hill lists it as a coin first struck by Valerian (1965: 289; pl. 34: 12), I have entertained the probability that the reading of . . . TRAIANVSAVG is a scribal error on that specimen, but as it stands, I first must list it as a coin of Decius Traianus.

A true first among the coins of Valerian is a specimen that showed up in our 1971 season at Khirbet Shemaᶜ (M71 1482; see pl. 16). On the obverse is the full legend of Valerian surrounding the radiate bust. On the reverse is partially nude Tyche standing with a cruciform standard in her right hand. To the goddess' left and our right is a pedestal with a little goddess atop that might be Nike. At the feet of Tyche is a murex shell and written around we read COLTYR [OMET]. The coin is a handsome bronze tetradrachma at 27 mm and 15.87 g.

In 1977 we discovered at Meiron a Tyrian coin of Valerian that depicts nude Apollo (?) with his right hand stretched over an incense altar at the left. There are two other tall objects at the right, one of which may be a palm tree (p. 66 below and pl. 15: M77 1240).

Gallienus (253-68 C.E.), son of Valerian, continued to strike a number of familiar coins, among them the following: (1) Astarte being crowned by Nike, (2) frontal view of the temple of Astarte, (3) the portable shrine with arched top and Astarte within, (4) the seated figure of Roma (begun by Valerian), (5) Nike advancing with wreath and palm branch, (6) the nude, standing figure of

Melqart/Herakles (begun by Valerian), (7) Kadmos hurling a rock at a serpent (begun by Gordian III), (8) Kadmos running on the deck of a galley, (9) the river-god (begun by Valerian), (10) the eagles standing with wings spread and the standard of the Third Legion (see the coins of Geta above), and (11) the agonistic table with two crowns atop (a type first done by Caracalla) (Hill 1965: 291-95).

Three new designs emerged. The first features Kadmos standing nude. He holds a spear and a chlamys in his left hand, a phial in his right. To our right we see a heifer lying at his feet. There is a city gate with towers above. Written beneath it is ΘH/BE; the murex shell is in left field (Hill 1965: 293; pl. 34: 18). The coin alludes to the founding of Thebes by the son of Europa.

The second new design also features Kadmos, draped to the waist and holding a spear transversely as he stands. He is handing a papyrus roll to three Hellenes at our left. In the exergue is written EΛΛH/NEC KAΔ/MOC. There is a murex shell at the left, at the feet of Kadmos (Hill 1965: 293; pl. 35: 1). It is interesting to see how, more and more, the story of Tyre's role among the nations of the Mediterranean at an earlier time was being celebrated on these 3rd-century coins. There may have been something of local pride at work here. There also may have been an increasing amount of interest in antiquity on the part of savants of the Roman world. I would judge that the 3rd century was a time of much intellectual curiosity that reflects itself here and in the lively amount of interest in novel religious ideas and religious syncretism. It is quite striking, from the standpoint of syncretism, that some of these coins bear both Latin and Greek script.

The third new design depicts a sacrifice to Melqart/Herakles by a female figure in a tall kalathos, long chiton, and himation. She stands with both arms raised above a flaming altar. The entire scene is before a distyle temple seen from quarter perspective and containing the club of Herakles (Hill 1965: 294). The reverse inscriptions read COL TVRO METR or COL TVRO MET. So also the reverse inscriptions of Salonina that follow.

For Salonina, wife of Gallienus, six coin reverses were struck. Four are continuations of previously used motifs—(1) Hermes/Thoth as on a coin of Volusianus, (2) Kadmos hurling a stone at a serpent, (3) Okeanos reclining (as on a coin of Valerian), and (4) the four-legged agonistic table with two prize crowns. One of the new types is only a variant of the last. It depicts an agonistic table with three rather than four legs (Hill 1965: 295-96; pl. 35: 6).

The other new coin shows two figures of Nike standing side by side, each with a wreath in her right hand and a palm branch in the left. The murex shell is in left field (Hill 1965: 295).

With this the coins of the City of Tyre come to an end. The sons of Gallienus and Salonina took the throne, one succeeding another after their parents were murdered. The next years were tumultuous for the empire. There was no strong hand at the helm until the accession of Aurelian (270-75 c.e.), whose strength was probably matched by Probus (276-82 c.e.) and increased by Diocletian (284-305 c.e.). Times were not easy for the emperors. Entire populations of the empire were restive. Various features of older ways were giving way to new or to nothing. Coinage had ceased in other cities. Now it was forced to cease at Tyre.

Judging from the ruins of the Roman era, we must say that Tyre was still an impressive city. It boasted one of the largest and finest hippodromes in the empire, as well as a number of fine public buildings. Its citizens and the empire had invested much in that city, and the returns had been handsome. Even the coins of Tyre indicate this, for while the imperial coinage suffered more and more from inflation, the Tyrian bronze coins had remained large and substantial to the end. Had this itself been too much of an embarrassment to the empire? Perhaps Gallienus decided that such systems of coinage would have to be eliminated in order to restore credibility in the imperial money. We do not know. There are no historical documents that tell us of any such decision. Scholars are able to describe what happened, but none can give a sure explanation.[7] One can only consider the components of the general economic problems of the Roman Empire and surmise from that. Inflationary problems only continued after this point. Even the attempt to save the staggering antoniani by coating them with silver as they were issued did nothing. That coin, which was the mainstay of imperial coinage throughout the mid-3rd century, finally had to give way to a new series of coppers in the time of Diocletian and the confession that money is not necessarily worth its own weight in the metal of which it is made. Imperial decree alone dictated its value.

One must say that it is quite remarkable that the city coinage of Tyre held out as long as it did, for it was one of the last to go. From the time that Septimius Severus declared the city a colony (201 C.E.?) until sometime in the reign of Gallienus and Salonina (253-60 C.E.),[8] the city's officials assured the striking of impressively large copper coins, rough in texture to be sure, but thick and heavy. Some of these coins attain a weight of 27 g, which is a size that suggests the sestertius of earlier times. More commonly, the larger coins weigh ca. 23 g, while smaller sizes weigh ca. 15, 9.5, and 6 g, respectively.[9] While this situation continued at Tyre and at a few other places, the imperial coinage had suffered only progressive degeneration. Beginning with the reign of Septimius Severus the silver content of silver coins was cut first to 65%, and by the year 220, to 45%. By the year 238 the content of the denarius was down to 30%, and it ceased to be struck. In what may have been an effort to rescue the failing denarius, Caracalla instituted the coin we call the antonianus. Though it was supposed to represent a double-denarius, it was, in fact, only about one and one-half times the size of the trusted coin. The silver content of the antonianus so rapidly declined that by mid-century it has all the appearance of a copper coin. At about 260 C.E. Gallienus issued antoniani covered with silver wash, but the public was not long deceived by this, and the effort failed to regenerate confidence in the imperial economy. Within a decade after that the antonianus was no more than small change. At new weight it was a copper of about 3.5 g—a stingy replacement for the handsome colonial coppers of Tyre that so suddenly had ceased to be struck!

It is easy enough to guess at the cause of the empire-wide inflation if one speaks in the most general terms. It was part of what we have come to call, all too nonchalantly, the decline of the Roman Empire (after Gibbons' famed multivolume work with that phrase in its title, of course). Michael Grant, a numismatist, has been most specific in identifying the cause quite simply as the impoverishing wars of the period. He states that defensive wars could have been afforded, but it was the aggressive wars that did the damage in that they demanded unreasonably high pay-offs for the army (1968: 247). Richard Reece, another numismatist, cites two factors: frantic wars and incompetent emperors (1970: 22). Both of these simplifications must be correct, but the total situation was so complicated that only a team of trained economists working together with historians and with reams of data at their disposal could come near an adequate answer. Unfortunately, most of the information we would need for such an adequate analysis can no longer be retrieved. Without it, one must simply begin with a point of view and proceed to make observations from it. This is what Gibbon did in the 18th century, using the classical sources that were known to him and are still available to us. Indeed, we might do well to review some of his observations.

Gibbon began by pointing out that the 3rd century was inaugurated by an emperor who was of aristocratic origin. Septimius Severus was a man who rose through the military ranks and even disdained senatorial status when it was offered to him. By doing that he set a precedent for a new base of power on the part of emperors. In the 3rd century, more than in the two centuries prior or even in the century that succeeded, the way to the emperor's throne was by force and support of the army. This, in turn, was an expensive way, for the support of the soldiers had to be purchased with liberal donations.

In his treatment of Caracalla, Gibbon pointed to his profligate spending and wastage of human resources. Nor was Caracalla the only emperor to act that way. The dozens who pretended to the throne and those who succeeded in putting them down used the same means. Most of the augustae of the 3rd century earned their positions at the expense of much blood and much money.

The erosion of respect for the constitution and the values it stood for was noted by Gibbon more than once. Thus it was that he could praise Decius for his attempts to "restore public virtue, ancient principles and manners, and the oppressed majesty of the laws" (Gibbon 1936: vol. 1, p. 242). Another way to look at this would be to say that with more and more emperors coming from the provinces, there was less and less understanding of old Roman values.

All would agree, perhaps, that the constant inroads of the Goths and other barbarians at the borders was a huge factor in the decline of the empire. What this had to do with the weakening of the economy is harder to discover— beyond the mere cost of holding them at bay. These groups attacked as they did partly *because of* the growing weakness of the empire. They were like wolves after an old moose because it has much meat and subsiding power to defend itself. It is after all the tired, old prey rather than the young and hearty that attracts the jaws of the predators. This was as much a result of as it was a cause for the border wars. Add to this the constant pressures of the Persians to the east and the civil disorders in Sicily, Alexandria, and Asia Minor, and the picture is one of siege at every side and within. The old empire was becoming a sitting goose in the eyes of many who desired independence, power, or its wealth.

All of this described by Gibbon is as much a description of symptoms as a naming of causes. One might have to settle for simply saying that the institution was becoming increasingly weak and disorganized in its old age—but then marvel at how much longer it survived beyond the crises of the 3rd century. It continued as an empire into the 5th century, albeit in altered form.

It should be emphasized that monetary inflation was one of many symptoms of the diseased body and that it was accompanied by a similar inflation of other values. Just as a silver coin was no longer what it once had been, so it was a much lighter thing to be an emperor. Those who tried were a proverbial dime a dozen, so it seemed, and those who were hastily put in office at the tragic death of an incumbent tended to be unimpressive. Both wealth and power were more a matter of luck and cruel force than of something patiently earned. That, as much as anything, might be a definition of inflation, for inflation is what we have when it becomes too easy to earn what only appears to be great. Inflation is partly brought on when those who initially have the wealth are forced to share it with those who do not and who, in sharing, deliberately inflate the gift to make it look bigger than it actually is. This is precisely what many emperors and pretenders did in order to buy the support of their armies. In time, the recipients catch on to this, of course, and they simply demand more. As this continues, they eventually exhaust the source, and even he who had it to begin with finds himself impoverished.

We have information to indicate that there were colonies like Tyre that did not share in all the sufferings the empire endured. While the empire continued to weaken, Tyre and other cities like it held strong. Even when the governing powers of Tyre were forced to cease striking coins, this situation most likely continued for a time. Nonetheless, the city remained an important center of commerce,[10] and, in a sense as much religious as political, the pride of the city stayed strong.[11]

The source and nature of that pride is registered most accurately in the 3rd-century coins that we have described. There are various elements in the iconography that can be isolated into distinct and separate themes, and in those themes we can see something of what was going on. A review of these coins cannot but impress a viewer for the sheer variety of types. In the brief reign of a single emperor one can find, as in the case of Valerian, 14 distinct reverses plus another 6 for his wife.

The chief distinction between the Tyrian coins of the 3rd century and those that precede is this: for more than three centuries' worth of autonomous coinage, we see only four basic designs with variations. In the 3rd century, from 201 to 268, we see a total of 51 reverse designs. The Roman emperors were notorious for their introduction of reverse designs and mottos on their coins and for variations of them. This is because they viewed the coins as a most effective way to propagate their ideas and ambitions. Given the limitations of communication media of the time, the coin was the quickest route to the eye and mind of the population at large. Its pictures and legends circulated what the emperors wanted the armies and the population to know about their plans and policies. Nor was this use of the coin restricted to the imperial coinage. Here at Tyre, as an example of one city, the coins were used to advertise both religious and political ideas. The only thing left for us to wonder is whether they communicate mostly for the emperor and his court or for the local leadership.

One set of symbols on these coins is traditionally Tyrian or Phoenician. This set includes the murex shell, the goddess Astarte, the palm tree or palm branch, the unique club of Melqart/Herakles and to a certain extent Melqart himself, and the galley. These symbols represent what Tyre was in view of its own history and talents.

Astarte was featured from near the beginning of the series to the very end. A temple to the ancient goddess must have been an important building in the city of Tyre. Its facade is pictured for us on many coins and the scene within that facade on many more. Though the temple of Herakles/Melqart had seemed more important to the Macedonian conqueror, Astarte's temple turned out to be more important in the minds of the natives, I would surmise.

It is interesting to see that the murex shell is present on the greatest number of coin reverses. It is almost always in a subordinate position, to be sure, but it is persistently there. The literary sources support the importance of the purple-dye industry just as emphatically, as we noted in the review of Tyre's history. To the outside world and to the native, Tyre was most famed for this industry.

Through such symbols we see strong continuity between the different periods of history that are so neatly divided into pre-Alexandrian, Ptolemaic, Seleucid, autonomous, and Roman by the very coins themselves. There were certain elements and religious figures that remained Tyrian through all those periods.

Related to this set of symbols is another group that would seem to be purely Tyrian but are not. They are the scenes and characters that represent legendary accounts of the founding of both Tyre and Carthage, the founding of Thebes, and the bearing of the alphabet from Phoenicia to the Greeks. The legends may not even be originally Tyrian. They were legends about Tyre and other Phoenicians that were known by Greeks and others. The tale of the "ambrosial rocks" is attributed to a Phoenician source but even that is a tale that may have been best known to Greeks. Dido and Kadmos (the name is from *qdm* and denotes "the easterner") are characters from Greek tales. They extol the tradition of Tyre, but they do it from the perspective of outside admirers. They pay tribute to Tyre more than they express native pride. Indeed, it may have been the Hellenistic elements in the Tyrian population that most loved these stories. It is notable that the number of coins bearing these motifs increased through the middle of the 3rd century.

Perhaps this is a phenomenon that can be observed generally throughout the world and through all of history. A group of migrants moves, for example, to Australia. In order to acquire territory they must push aside or annihilate some or much of the native population. Yet once they are established, the immigrants and their offspring become Australian. They adopt local symbols as their own and even fancy themselves to be natives. One can observe this phenomenon repeatedly in the countries of the western hemisphere. As violent as the white invaders could be in grabbing land and other resources from the native population, there comes a day when their descendants and even first-generation migrants lay claim to some features of the native traditions.

The 3rd century was a time of religious and cultural syncretism and the 3rd-century coins of Tyre illustrate the truth of that as well. Yet more than that, those coins reveal the particular character of the city itself minus the Christian influence that was there. They demonstrate that the important citizens of Tyre identified themselves as Tyrians and Hellenes. They were, at the same time, proud to be a full-fledged colony of Rome, and they were open to the ideas and movements that traveled freely in the eastern Mediterranean at that time. Their city was in the mainstream of popular thought and fads. Tyrian pride resisted some of it, but that was hardly for lack of awareness. The absence of Christian motifs in the coins, while Christianity was actually gaining strength in the city, is proof of that. It was a cosmopolitan city, but the cosmopolitan elements were arranged around a core of strong and tenacious city pride that was rooted in ancient traditions and ancient sources of wealth.

Judging from the evidence before us, a great many influences must have been present at Tyre. The Greek presence is undeniable, but it is a Greek presence that admires what is native to the city and its territory. The importance of Tyre as a great colonizer and a great trader with Greeks was magnified to the point of being legendary.

A third group of symbols represents Hellenistic influence most purely. These symbols range from such a mixing of elements as the composite figure of Melqart/Herakles to the truly Greek idea of the Heraklean games and the prize crowns that went with them. The temples depicted on the coins show this Greek influence as well, not least of all the Phoenician temple of the Koinon. Tyche, the protectress of the city, is Greek in form and style. So are Dionysos, Apollo, and Okeanos. Hermes/Thoth represents popular Greek syncretism.

Roman elements are often hard to delineate because there are so many features that are best termed Greco-Roman; Nike is an example. She is Greek in character, but the idea of Nike presenting a crown to Astarte seems to be quite Roman. The Romans thought that way about gods and goddesses. More clearly Roman is the figure of Harmonia standing with Kadmos in one of the coins of Philip. The tributes to the Third Legion are Roman, but not purely Roman because some of the symbols are either local or from other sources. Because of Virgil's compositions, the representation of the founding of Carthage by Dido can be considered Roman in part. The eagle represented imperial Rome, but it was Ptolemaic before that, and in the east, it could represent the sun. More Roman than any of these is the first coin in the series, the coin of Septimius Severus that depicts the founding of the colony, with ox, cow, plowman, and plow in the fashion that was native to Roman culture. Severus was laying his claim as one who thought himself Roman. Adding the symbol of the Third Legion advertised his military position. He was the Roman conqueror leaving token of his powers at a place from which he could control the region around. Tyre was strategic, and he made it to be even more so by this move.

Most Roman of all is the image on the obverses of the coins. Tyrian autonomy could be demonstrated on the reverses. The obverses were reserved for the imperial image. Even provincial and colonial coins were a vehicle for this political claim. Rome was truly mistress over her many provinces and colonies.

A fourth set of symbols could be termed miscellaneous in that they originate from here and there; but because they represent something important by way of the religious temper of the age, we can call them the symbols of the new religions. Not that they were without ancient roots, for they were deeply rooted in old traditions, but they represent religious movements in vogue at the time. I have in mind such symbols as the sacred stone, the river- or lake-god, the shrines that are depicted, perhaps even the bull who was mascot to the Gallian Legion. Only the symbols of Christianity are missing. Perhaps it was a threat to the syncretistic temper of the ruling group.

## NOTES

[1]See Hill 1965: 271 and pl. 33: 13. Other designs were used to commemorate the games. This same basic design recurs on coins of Gallienus and his wife, Salonina. In Jidejian (1969: 103-4) we read the following information concerning these games: "During the . . . French excavation campaign a Greek inscription on a fragment of grey marble column was found at Tyre. It states that a certain Eutychos, a native of Ephesus, *pantathlos*, was the victor in the Acta Heraclia games. . . . During the third century A.D. every four years the Heraclia games were solemnly held. . . . Other festivals held at Tyre at regular intervals were the Olympia and Commodia games."

[2]We found an example of this at Meiron in 1974. It is likely the same coin as that of Julia Domna noted above (Hill 1965: 270; pl. 32: 8).

[3]There are coins of Emesa that depict the great altar of Elagabal (Helios of Gebal) and of his temple. Consult the British Museum's *Catalogue of the Greek Coins of Galatia, Cappadocia and Syria* (London, 1899) for examples. The temple has six columns across the front. In the middle is the sun-stone with an eagle in front of it.

[4]According to Jidejian (1969: 99) the excavations at Tyre have failed to yield any remains that can be identified as the temple of Astarte.

[5]The figure of Kadmos became increasingly popular in Tyrian iconography, though this particular design was not repeated. Herodotus tells the tale of Kadmos in The Legend of Apollodorus. According to the tale, Kadmos set out to find Europa who had been abducted by Zeus. An oracle told him to follow a cow and build a city where the cow lay down. Thebes in Boeotia was the site where the cow directed him, and there he built that city. Among the gifts that he brought with him to Greece was the alphabet.

[6]Perhaps the reading of these coins should be HPAK IA O VM IA A WNEI. Not having a specimen at hand, I can do no more than suggest this as a possibility.

[7]Daniel Sperber, who has made a study of this, can point out that it was no longer profitable to strike these large coppers in the face of the inflated cost of the material. The alternative would have been to abandon gold and silver in exchange for copper as a base. Sperber (1970: 4-5) states, "It is clear that there was no imperial edict ordering the closure of these local mints, for they do not all stop their activities at the same time. There are in fact some half a dozen instances of cities in Pamphylia and Pisidia issuing local bronze coins as late as Claudius II, Aurelian and, in one case, Tacitus. It seems probable that it gradually became less economic for the cities to produce the local bronze pieces as the antonianus dropped in value. Or in other words 'their value as bullion exceeded

the value assigned to them by the mint, and under such conditions they would not be minted.' (The source of the quotation is unclear.) The fact that the modules tend to get larger in the mid III cent [sic] may well be a sign of copper inflation and not of prosperity. Certainly by the end of Aurelian's reign it would hardly have been worth while issuing local bronze denominations. . . . Why some cities did nonetheless continue issuing bronze is still something of a puzzle, but there may have been localised reasons—strong conservative traditions?—for this.

"This local copper coinage had undoubtedly acted as a stabilizing influence during the earlier part of the century, and the extent of its increase, most especially in the 40's, is clearly indicative of the strong demand for a stable currency. Thus, confidence in the ant. must have been wavering very considerably. When this source of 'stable currency' dried up, it should have been matched by comparable emissions of some equally stable currency—in gold. The fact that there is no evidence of 'absolute shortage of gold during Gallienus' period' (West) is not enough. In order to satisfy the obvious demand for stable currency, there should have been a significant rise in gold emission and circulation, one relatively comparable to the bronze boom. But there is no evidence of this.

"Furthermore, yet another potentially stabilizing element had been taken off the market, probably during the latter years of Decius. For it appears both from hoard evidence and from certain legal texts that c. 250 all the earlier silver denarii in circulation were officially demonetized and, no doubt, bought up by the government."

[8] It was in ca. 260 that Gallienus began to strike the silver-coated antoniani according to some sources (cf. Reece 1970: 37). Was this also the year when city coinage ceased at Tyre? It is possibly so.

[9] Reece (1970: 132) refers to these as "the large copper drachm, and occasional issues of its half, quarter and eighth."

[10] Jidejian (1969: 91-92) states, "In spite of religious conflict Tyre continued to prosper because of her industries and commerce. In the reign of Diocletian (A.D. 284-305) a certain Dorotheus found favor with the emperor and was honored by being placed at the head of the purple dye factories in the city. . . . In addition to the purple dye industry, Tyre was considered one of the important commercial centers for linen. . . . Another industry of Tyre was the manufacture of glass. Although Sidon was the chief seat of the industry, good sand was also found near Tyre. At Tyre the traces of the industry are less extensive but on the other hand archaeological evidence has proved that during the Byzantine and Arab periods glass manufacture still flourished." Fleming (1915) provides more details. We quote several excerpts. "In the midst of intellectual strife and religious unrest, Tyre continued to prosper because of her manufacturing and commerce. Rome seems to have assumed control of the purple dyeing industries of the city" (p. 75). "Late in the year 312 A.D. after Constantine's victory over Maxentius, the Edict of Milan was issued by Constantine and Licinius, announcing religious liberty for all and the right of 'every man to perform his religious duties according to his own choice' (Eusebius). With the edict there seems to have been sent forth a letter of instructions to the local authorities as to the carrying out of its provisions. Such a letter addressed to Anulinus, Proconsul of Africa, has come down to us. Among its provisions it orders that restoration be made to the Christian churches of all that had been taken away from them in the times of persecution, 'whether gardens, buildings, or whatever they might be' (Eusebius). It was immediately following the issuing of this edict that the work of building the temple of Tyre began. By the zeal of Paulinus, Bishop of Tyre, this temple was built. It was the most splendid in Phoenicia" (p. 76). "In 335 A.D., under Constantine, Tyre was chosen as the seat of a Church council. . . ." (p. 77). "Tyre was in a flourishing condition in the days of Jerome (340-420). He finds difficulty in reconciling Ezekiel's prophecy of the destruction of Tyre with the condition of the city in his own time" (p. 78).

[11] Fleming (1915: 75) states, "The city was the scene of bloody persecutions in the reign of Diocletian and Maximinus. Although Christianity had numbered great leaders among its adherents at Tyre, the ancient faith of the city was far from being dead."

# CHAPTER 4
## COINS FROM THE UPPER GALILEE

During the summers of 1970-72, 1974-75, and 1977-78, the author was involved in excavations at the Upper Galilean sites of Khirbet Shema$^c$, Meiron, and Gush Ḥalav. Directing the initial excavations at the site of Khirbet Shema$^c$ were Eric M. Meyers of Duke University, A. Thomas Kraabel of the University of Minnesota, and James F. Strange of the University of South Florida in Tampa, with G. Ernest Wright as Project Overseer and Robert J. Bull as Senior Archeological Advisor. That entire expedition has been reported in the volume prepared by the staff, *Ancient Synagogue Excavations at Khirbet Shema$^c$, Upper Galilee, Israel 1970-72* (published for the American Schools of Oriental Research by Duke University, 1976). Excavations at Meiron were begun in 1971. The seasons of 1971-72 and 1974-75 became Meiron Expedition Project Phase I. Meiron Phase II was begun in 1977 and includes work at the lower synagogue site of Gush Halav, which is ca. 6 km north of Meiron itself. Preliminary reports of Meiron were published in *BASOR* 214 (April 1974: 2-24) and 221 (February 1976: 93-101). A final publication is now in progress. Senior staff for the Meiron projects include Eric M. Meyers as Director, James F. Strange as Associate Director, Carol L. Meyers of Duke University as Field Archeologist, the author as numismatist, and Dennis E. Groh of Garrett-Evangelical Theological Seminary as ceramist.

As numismatist, I had to clean and identify the coins we have unearthed, to study them and to bring them to final publication form. The task has not been easy, for the corpus of coins includes Greek types from the 3rd century B.C.E. onward, Jewish coins of the Hasmonean era and the 1st century C.E., Roman imperial coins and various city and provincial coins of the Roman era, Byzantine, and, finally, Islamic coins. It is impossible to be master of all these types, of course. At times I have struggled on my own; at other times I have used the assistance of the American Numismatic Society in New York. In the end, all responsibility is mine no matter how numerous are the beginner's mistakes that appear in print.

There have been some intriguing corpora among the nearly 4,000 coins we have found to date at our three sites. Greatest in number are the Late Roman coins that come from the 4th-century-C.E. levels of dwelling that predominate at all three sites. They are all common types, however, and therefore, not particularly exciting to numismatists or collectors. Second greatest in number have been the Jewish coins of the Hasmonean era, most frequently coins of Alexander Jannaeus. Often as not, these coins are found together with Roman coins of the 4th century C.E.—a fact which had caused considerable puzzlement until we found increasing evidence of the presence of those coins in Jewish hands at that date. Thanks to a single hoard found at Gush Halav in 1977, we now also have a large corpus of Roman coins from the 5th century C.E.[1] Except for a goodly number of *antoniani* from the last half of the 3rd century C.E., Roman imperial coins are relatively sparse from the time of Roman conquest to the reign of Valerian, and most of the supply for that era came from local mints. Most interesting of all to myself has been the strong presence of Phoenician coins at our sites and, most especially, coins struck at the city of Tyre. Standing out from all the other local points of supply, Tyre contributed the greatest corpus of city coins we have unearthed at our Upper Galilee locations.

To put this in the larger perspective of our three excavations, I can report the following sample coin counts. Numbers are subject to some revision because of coins in barely legible condition and because my work with the Meiron and Gush Ḥalav coins is not yet completed. The categories I have chosen regard date periods as well as coin types.

| Period and type | Khirbet Shemaᶜ | Meiron | Gush Ḥalav |
|---|---|---|---|
| Persian era | | | 1 |
| Ptolemaic era | 4 | 2 | |
| Seleucid (Tyre) | 8 | 40 | 5 |
| Tyre (autonomous) | 18 | 96 | 8 |
| Sidon | | 1 | 1 |
| Gaza | | 1 | |
| Ptolemais-Acco | | 4 | |
| Hasmonean | 55 | 140 | 4 |
| Palestine under Roman rule | 4 | 33 | 2 |
| Roman Imperial, 1st-2nd centuries C.E. | 6 | 10 | 1 |
| Roman Colonial, 3rd century C.E. (city coins) | | | |
| Tyre | 5 | 25 | 4 |
| Aradus | | | 1 |
| Tripoli | | 1 | |
| Berytus | | 1 | |
| Acco | | 2 | |
| Petra | | 2 | |
| Bostra | 3 | 2 | |
| uncertain | | 7 | 2 |
| Roman Imperial, 3rd century C.E. (antoniani) | 10 | 41 | 5 |
| Late Roman (4th-early 5th century C.E.) | 361 | 567 | 161 |
| Byzantine | 6 | 1 | 3 |
| Islamic | 37 | 45 | |
| Totals | 517 | 1021 | 198 |

As one can readily see, all three sites produced a great quantity of Late Roman coins. The ratio of Hasmonean coins is quite high at Khirbet

Shema[c] and Meiron. Meiron produced the greatest variety of coins and the greatest number of coins representing the first three centuries C.E. These statistics are partly a matter of chance, of course. To swell the number of Late Roman coins from Meiron we excavated a single dwelling that turned up over 400 specimens. (I have omitted from the count the hoard found at Gush Halav. Of the 1961 coins in that hoard, 80% or more are of the 5th century C.E.) It must be significant that virtually no Byzantine coins and few Islamic specimens turned up in the sizable count from the Meiron site. All these statistics have much to do with periods and patterns of habitation at each of the respective sites, and the sites are by no means identical in that regard. The one noteworthy feature upon which I am focusing in this particular study is the presence of a sizable number of coins that were struck at Tyre from the 2nd century B.C.E. into the reign of Gallienus (253-68 C.E.). Except for the overwhelming supply of Hasmonean coins from the 1st century B.C.E., the coins from Tyre account for more than half of the supply for that period.[2] More precisely, I can state the following.

Our total supply of coins from the 2nd century B.C.E. consists of Seleucid dilepta minted at Tyre.

A steady, even supply of coins from Tyre continued through the 1st century B.C.E.

For the 1st century C.E., coins from Tyre account for almost half of our total supply. About half of the rest come from Palestine. Roman imperial and other local mints account for the remainder.[3]

For the 2nd century C.E., five-eighths of the total supply comes from Tyre. The rest are a mix of imperial and various local coins with the local coins dominating.[4]

The entire supply of coins for the first half of the 3rd century C.E. are from local mints, and a full half of those are from Tyre alone. Roman antoniani begin with the reign of Valerian and account for the total supply of coins until the time of Licinius when the new series of Roman coppers replaced them.

We can safely say, then, that the Tyrian mint was the chief supplier of money for the Upper Galilee for three and one-half centuries of that four and one-half century span of time. Only a huge supply of Hasmonean coins interrupts that balance.

This indicates two matters of economic interest. One is the fact that Tyre was a major supplier of money in the Levant. The other is the indication that Tyre was the center of economic influence for a peripheral area that included the Upper Galilee in its orbit.[5] The villagers of the Upper Galilee were marketing their oil and other products[6] in the direction of Tyre and receiving Tyrian money in return. Very few coins at our sites came from nearby mints to the south, such as the mint at Tiberias.

With this evidence in mind I have deemed it useful to publish this volume concerning Tyrian coins only from our three sites of Khirbet Shema[c], Meiron, and Gush Ḥalav. It is not that I have many new coins to introduce to the public, for only a handful of unusual coins turned up. It is merely that I want to produce a case study which supplements and rounds out what we already know of this one unique and somewhat important city of the Levant. By doing so I can call attention to several factors, chiefly economic and politico-religious, that can sharpen our understanding of the times in which this material was produced. By knowing what coins circulated in the Upper Galilee we can gain some notion of the kinds of coins that were most commonly used in a region like this some 50 km distant from the source. By paying attention to the symbols on those coins, we can gain further understanding of what was happening in Tyre itself.

With that I proceed to the presentation of our numismatic materials of Tyrian origin. I present it in chronological order for the most part. Only when I have desired to follow a certain series for its full course do I depart from that. The information I have given includes diameter, weight in grams, a description of the coin concerned, and the date. The code numbers at the left are a guide to our own registry. "KS" stands for Khirbet Shemaᶜ, "M" for Meiron, and "GH" for Gush Ḥalav. Because I have discussed bibliographical material in a previous section, I am not providing complete bibliographical references.


*Coins of the Ptolemaic Era*

Earliest among our coins are five specimens of the Ptolemaic era that are possibly, though not probably, from Tyre. One of them is brass; the other four are bronze. All are in worn condition. The weights range from 4.06 to 5.80 g; the diameters, from 16 to 18 mm. On the obverse of all is the bust of one who could be titled either Zeus/Amon Re or a bearded version of Melqart. The head is crowned with a lion's skin headdress. On the reverse is an eagle facing left with its wings open and a thunderbolt in its claws. On the two clearest specimens there appears to be a palm branch over the eagle's shoulder. The obverse of the second example is clearly like that of pl. 39: 18 in Hill (1965). One must observe, however, that our specimen is bronze while that is silver. The first specimen is less clear on the reverse in that no club is visible to the left. We present these two as coins of Tyre.


| KS71 1376 | Obv: Bearded bust facing right. | 3rd c. B.C.E. |
| 16 mm | Rev: Eagle with wings partially spread | |
| 5.80 g | facing our left, palm branch over its | |
| | shoulder. Inscribed around: [ΠΤΟΛΕ]- | |
| | ΜΑΙ[ΟΥ Β]ΑΣΙ[ΛΕΩΣ]. | |

| M75 128 | Obv: Badly corroded and worn but appar- | 3rd c. B.C.E. |
| 17 mm | ently the same as above. | |
| 4.16 g | Rev: Same as above, but with a war | |
| (pl. 1) | club at the left. Inscribed around: ΠΤΟΛ- | |
| | ΕΜΑΙ[ΟΥ] ΒΑΣΙΛ[ΕΩΣ]. | |

*Coins of the Seleucid Era, 202-126* B.C.E.

GH78 073            One silver coin of the Seleucid period came to light in the
                    1978 excavations at Gush Halav. The coin is 21 mm in
                    diameter and 6.63 g in weight. On the obverse is a heroic bust
                    of the king, and on the reverse we see the eagle with the palm
                    branch over his shoulder with AΣ̌ beneath the branch and
                    the date, ΓΙ, beneath the branch. At the left is the Tyrian war
                    club with P̌E above it, and around at the left we read
                    ANTIOXOY. In all details except for the date the coin is the
                    same as what we see in Rogers 1927: 21 and pl. 2. The date is
                    too low to fit in the Alexandrine series. It could represent the
                    13th of one of the Antiochuses. The only one who qualifies is
                    Antiochus III (223-187 B.C.E.), but that gives us a date too
                    early for a Tyrian series. Perhaps the 13th year of Seleucid
                    rule in Tyre is intended. If so, the date should be 189/8 B.C.E.

     We found the following bronze dilepta that were struck at Tyre
during the Seleucid period.

M72 2278            Obv: Bust of Antiochus III.                    202/1 B.C.E.
13 mm               Rev: Palm tree with fruit, date across
1.73 g              field as I P (110). Inscribed around:
                    [ . . . B]AΣIΛEΩΣ.

KS72 2194           Obv: Same bust as above.                       195/4 B.C.E.
13 mm               Rev: Same as above, with date as ZIP
2.20 g              (117).
(pl. 2)

KS71 1570           Obv: Same bust as above.                       202-187 B.C.E.
14 mm               Rev: Same as above, with AN[TIOXOY
3.32 g              BA]ΣIΛEΩΣ inscribed around.
(pl. 2)

GH77 1215           Obv: Bust of Antiochus IV with circle          175-164 B.C.E.
14-15 mm            of dots around.
2.83 g              Rev: Same as above, with ANTIOXOY
                    . . . inscribed around.

M75 342             Obv: Bust of Antiochus IV.                     175-164 B.C.E.
15 mm               Rev: Same as above, with ANTIO[XOY
2.56 g              . . . inscribed around.
(pls. 1, 2)

KS72 2134           Obv: Bust of Demetrius II (?) with circle      146-143 B.C.E.
13 mm               of dots around.
1.72 g              Rev: Same as above, with date as _ P
(pl. 2)             (16_). Inscribed around, . . . BAΣI-
                    Λ[EΩΣ].

| | | |
|---|---|---|
| KS71 1369<br>13 mm<br>1.77 g<br>(pl. 1) | Obv: Bust of Demetrius II.<br>Rev: Same as above, with date as HΞP<br>(168). Inscribed around, . . . ΒΑΣΙΛΕΩΣ. | 144/3 B.C.E. |
| KS71 1497<br>14 mm<br>1.84 g<br>(pl. 1) | Obv: Bust of Demetrius II.<br>Rev: Same as above. | 144/3 B.C.E. |
| M77 205<br>14 mm<br>2.12 g | Obv: Bust of Demetrius II (?).<br>Rev: Palm tree but with no inscriptional<br>material legible. | 146-138 B.C.E.? |
| M77 190<br>15 mm<br>1.77 g | Obv: Bust of Demetrius II (?).<br>Rev: Same as above. | 146-138 B.C.E.? |
| M77 257<br>12 mm<br>1.62 g | Obv: Bust of Demetrius II (?).<br>Rev: Unclear. | 146-138 B.C.E.? |
| M75 309<br>13 mm<br>1.28 g | Obv: Bust of Antiochus VII (?).<br>Rev: Palm tree with inscription around,<br>AN[TIOXOY . . . ]. Circle around all. | 138-129 B.C.E.? |
| M75 148<br>15 mm<br>1.57 g | Obv: Bust of Antiochus VII (?).<br>Rev: Palm tree with inscription around,<br>ANT[IOXOY B]ΑΣΙΛΕ[ΩΣ]. | 138-129 B.C.E.? |

The following are coins with a Seleucid bust on the obverse and a palm tree on the reverse but with no legible inscriptional material. All should be dated at 201-125 B.C.E.

| | | |
|---|---|---|
| KS 72 2256<br>14 mm<br>2.18 g | M74 144<br>12 mm<br>1.44 g<br>(pl. 1) | M75 291<br>12 mm<br>1.17 g<br>(pl. 1) |
| M77 1362<br>14-16 mm<br>2.21 g | GH77 1198<br>13 mm<br>2.17 g | GH78 057<br>14 mm<br>1.73 g |

There are 30 specimens of the type described above that are very badly worn. One can make out the Seleucid bust on the obverses and/or the palm tree on the reverses. Because they are badly worn, I have not given the weights. All should be dated, as above, to the period of 201-125 B.C.E. Registry numbers are as follows: KS70 567, KS71 1366, KS71 1443, KS72 2326, M71 2045, M72 2085, M72 2084, M72 2165, M72 2225, M72 2229, M72 2238, M72 2252, M72 2287, M74 004, M74 101, M74 408, M74 409, M75 071, M75 091, M75 178, M75 191, M75 192, M75 213, M75 290, M75 362, M77 1042, M77 1103, M77 1175, M77 1227, GH77 1276.

One lepton was found, with the Tyrian war club clear on the reverse but all other details worn beyond recognition. The other data are as follows.

M77 1300                                                       201-125 B.C.E.
9 mm
0.99 g

*The Autonomous Period: the Melqart/Palm Tree Series (Ae)*

M74 100          Obv: Bust of Melqart.                        99-54 B.C.E.?
22 mm            Rev: Palm tree with ΙΕΡΑΣ beneath.
9.22 g

*The Autonomous Period: the Tyche/War Galley Series (Ae)*

M74 146          Obv: Bust of Tyche.                          113/2 B.C.E.
15 mm            Rev: Galley with Astarte in it standing
1.65 g           to left, cruciform standard at left. In field
                 at right, L I(?). Below, *lṣr b.*

KS72 2215        Same as above, but very worn. No date        113-97 B.C.E.
16 mm            legible.
3.78 g

M74 237          Obv: Bust of Tyche.                          98/7 B.C.E.-
18 mm            Rev: Galley moving left, details worn        84/5 C.E.
5.55 g           away. Faint trace of ΙΕΡΑΣ above.
(pl. 3)

M75 194          Same as above, but with only a portion       "
22 mm            of the inscription legible.
5.19 g

M77 102          Same as above, with *lṣr* below.             "
18 mm
6.58 g

KS71 1379        Same as above, but very worn.                "
18 mm
4.40 g

M77 1362         Obv: Bust of Tyche.                          93-196 C.E.
17 mm            Rev: Galley with inscription above,
5.27 g           [ΙΕΡΑΣ]/ΜΗΤΡΟ/ΠΟΛΕΩΣ.

M72 2145         Same as above, but with the inscription      "
17 mm            including the Tyrian monogram plus
3.75 g           ΙΕΡΑ[C]/ΜΗΤΡΟΠ[Ο]/ΛΕWC.
(pl. 3)

GH78 194        Obv: Same as above, but with . . . ΙΕΡΑΣ/
20 mm           ΜΗΤΡΟΠΟ/ΛΕΩΣ *Isr* above the galley.
4.15 g

M72 2292        Same as above, but with only IEPAC          93-196 C.E.
13 mm           visible as a portion of the reverse inscrip-
6.05 g          tion.


The following have the size and texture of the above coins but with only
Tyche visible on the obverse and a galley on the reverse. They are very worn.
I would guess that they are all Tyrian.

M75 149         Brass and flattened to an irregular shape.
20-24 mm
3.06 g

| KS71 1372 | KS71 1416 | KS72 2195 | M72 2277 |
| 18 mm | 21 mm | 21 mm | 16 mm |
| 4.59 g | 3.94 g | 4.94 g | 5.06 g |
| M71 1483 | M72 2203 | M72 2258 | M72 2308 |
| 16 mm | 17 mm | 19 mm | 20 mm |
| 3.05 g | 5.14 g | 7.38 g | 5.14 g |


Coin of base silver (billon).

M77 1385        Obv: Bust of Tyche.                          104/5 C.E.
12 mm           Rev: Galley with Astarte standing to left.
1.44 g          Across middle of field, ΛΣ (230), ᛗᛈ .

*The Autonomous Period: the Tyche/Palm Tree Series (Ae)*

M72 2130        Obv: Bust of Tyche within ring of dots.      120/19 or
15 mm           Rev: Palm tree with L ꝗ (Phoenician *waw*   106/5 B.C.E.
2.87 g          or *kap*, 6 or 20) at left, monogram at right
(pl. 4)         and IEP ΑΣ across field below it.

M72 2144        Obv: Same as above.                          75/4 B.C.E.
16 mm           Rev: Palm tree with AN (51) at left,
2.44 g          monogram at right and IEP ΑΣ across
(pl. 4)         field below it.

GH77 1275       Obv: Bust of Tyche.                          26/5 B.C.E.
16 mm           Rev: Palm tree with ᴬᴿΣ at right, P (100)
3.33 g          at left.
(pl. 5)

KS72 2093       Same as above, with only a portion of        26/5 B.C.E.-
13 mm           the date visible as ..P (100 plus).           74/5 C.E.
3.43 g

| M75 475<br>16 mm<br>2.33 g<br>(pl. 5) | Obv: Bust of Tyche.<br>Rev: Palm tree with date about trunk in field, ΛΣ (230), inscription around as monogram plus ΜΗΤΡΟΠΟΛΕΩΣΙΕ-ΡΑΣ. | 104/5 C.E. |
|---|---|---|
| KS72 2266<br>16 mm<br>2.50 g<br>(pl. 4) | Same as above, but with date as ΔΛΣ (234) and portion of the inscription around reading monogram plus Μ[ΗΤ-ΡΟΠΟΛΕΩ]Σ ΙΕΡΑΣ. | 108/9 C.E. |
| M74 144<br>15-16 mm<br>3.05 g | Obv: Bust of Tyche.<br>Rev: Palm tree with fruit, date across field as ΔΛΣ (234). Around from left upwards, monogram plus [ΜΗΤΡΟΠΟΛΕΩΣΙ]Ε-ΡΑΣ. | 108/9 C.E. |
| M74 051<br>15 mm<br>4.26 g | Obv: Bust of Tyche.<br>Rev: Palm tree with fruit, date across field as ΓΜС (243). Around from left upwards, [monogram] plus ΜΗΤΡ[ΟΠΟΛΕ]WС-ΙΕΡΑС. | 117/8 C.E. |
| M77 1041<br>16 mm<br>3.82 g<br>(pl. 5) | Obv: Bust of Tyche.<br>Rev: Palm tree with fruit, date across field as ΖΜ С (247). Around from left upwards, ΙΕΡΑΣ plus monogram plus ΜΗΤΡΟΠΟΛΙС.[7] | 121/2 C.E. |
| M77 1045<br>16 mm<br>2.95 g<br>(pl. 5) | Obv: Bust of Tyche.<br>Rev: Palm tree with fruit, date across field as ΟΣ (270). Around from left upwards, monogram plus ΜΗΤΡΟΠ[ΟΛΕΩΣΙΕ-ΡΑΣ]. | 134/5 C.E. |
| KS70 522<br>14 mm<br>2.00 g | Same as above, but with only ΙΕΡΑΣ legible in the inscription. | 104-67 C.E. |
| KS71 1466<br>16 mm<br>3.43 g | Same as above, but with all of the inscription illegible. | 104-67 C.E. |

The following specimens are very worn. All that one can determine is the bust of Tyche on the obverse and the palm tree on the reverse. I must date them all to the broad range of 1st century B.C.E. to 167 C.E.

| KS70 608<br>15 mm<br>1.80 g | KS71 2041<br>12 mm<br>1.75 g | KS71 1512<br>13 mm<br>1.78 g | M77 1337<br>12 mm<br>2.40 g |
|---|---|---|---|

KS71  1411          KS72  2326          M71  1463          M77  1350
15 mm               12 mm               14 mm              14 mm
2.64 g              (broken)            0.94 g             3.10 g

M74  007            M74  088
12 mm               13 mm
2.03 g              2.77 g

## The Autonomous Period: the Melqart/War Club Series (Ae)

| | | |
|---|---|---|
| KS72 2073<br>22 mm<br>7.61 g<br>(pl. 6) | Obv: Bust of Melqart.<br>Rev: Club downward within oak leaf wreath, border of dots around. The major portion of the legend is worn away but at the bottom we can read the date PK (120) plus lṣr in Phoenician characters. | 6/5 B.C.E. |
| M71 1465<br>23 mm<br>12.04 g<br>(pl. 6) | Obv: Laureate, beardless bust of Melqart.<br>Rev: Club downward within oak leaf wreath, border of dots around. Tyrian monogram atop the club. Inscription across field as MH TPO/ΠΟΛ EWΣ/ HΛI (248) lsr. | 122/3 C.E. |
| KS71 1376<br>22 mm<br>11.78 g<br>(pl. 7) | Obv: Same as above.<br>Rev: Same as above, with inscription as [MHTPO]/ΠΟΛ [EWΣ]/HO[Σ] (278).<br>. . . | 152/3 C.E. |
| KS72 2064<br>20 mm<br>8.64 g | Obv: Same as above.<br>Rev: Same as above, with inscription as [MHTPO]/ΠΟΛ EWΣ/AΠΣ (281). . . . | 155/6 C.E. |
| KS72 2312<br>21 mm<br>9.87 g<br>(pl. 7) | Obv: Same as above.<br>Rev: Same as above, with inscription as MH TPO/ΠΟΛ EWΣ/AΠΣ (281) lṣr. | " |
| M72 2274<br>21 mm<br>8.31 g | Obv: Same as above.<br>Rev: Same as above, with inscription as MH TPO/ΠΟΛ EWΣ/AΠΣ (281) lṣr. | " |
| M72 2224<br>21 mm<br>8.02 g<br>(pl. 6) | Obv: Same as above.<br>Rev: Same as above. | " |
| M71 1467<br>21 mm<br>10.00 g<br>(pl. 7) | Obv: Same as above.<br>Rev: Same as above. | " |

| M72 2232<br>24 mm<br>10.25 g<br>(pl. 7) | Obv: Same as above.<br>Rev: Same as above, with inscription as<br>MH TPO/ΠOΛ EWΣ/. . . . | 98-156 C.E. |
|---|---|---|
| M74 141<br>21 mm<br>7.86 g | Obv: Same as above.<br>Rev: Club downward within wreath.<br>Across top and continuing across field,<br>TYPOY/MH TPO/ΠOΛ EWC/HT (308)<br>*lṣr.* | 182/3 C.E. |
| M75 181<br>21 mm<br>9.61 g<br>(pl. 8) | Obv: Same as above.<br>Rev: Same as above, with inscription as<br>TYPOY/MH T[PO]/ΠOΛ EW[C]/HT<br>*lṣr.* | " |
| M75 388<br>22 mm<br>5.79 g | Obv: Same as above.<br>Rev: Same as above, with inscription as<br>TY[POY]/MH TP[O]/ΠOΛ [E]W[C]/<br>HT *lṣr.* | " |
| M71 1578<br>23 mm<br>8.51 g | Obv: Same as above.<br>Rev: Same as above, with inscription as<br>TYPOY/MH TPO/ΠOΛ EWC/HT *lṣr.* | " |
| M72 2228<br>22 mm<br>7.06 g | Obv: Same as above.<br>Rev: Same as above, with inscription as<br>TYPOY/MH TPO/ΠOΛ EWC/HT<br>(308) *lṣr.* | 182/3 C.E. |
| M75 415<br>23 mm<br>8.31 g | Obv: Same as above.<br>Rev: Same as above, with inscription as<br>TYPOY/MH TPO/ΠOΛ EWC/ΘT<br>(309) *lṣr.* | 183/4 C.E. |
| KS70 578<br>21 mm<br>6.62 g | Obv: Same as above.<br>Rev: Same as above, with inscription as<br>TYPOY/MH TPO/ΠOΛ EWC/.T (30_)<br>*lṣr.* | 174-84 C.E. |
| M77 1288<br>23 mm<br>8.10 g | Obv: Same as above.<br>Rev: Same as above, with inscription as<br>TYPOY/MH TPO/ΠOΛ [EWC]/. . . . | 112-84 C.E. |
| M71 1449<br>22 mm<br>8.03 g | Obv: Same as above.<br>Rev: Same as above, with inscription as<br>MYPOY/MH TPO/ΠOΛ [EWC]/. . . . | " |
| M71 1422<br>23 mm<br>7.01 g | Obv: Same as above.<br>Rev: Same as above, with inscription as<br>TYPO[Y]/MH TPO/ΠOΛ EWC/. . . . | " |

M72 2200          Obv: Same as above.                                              "
22 mm             Rev: Same as above, with inscription as
9.50 g            TYP[OY]/MH TPO/ΠΟΛ E[WC]/. . . .

   The following are very worn coins that display only Melqart on the obverse
and a club on the reverse. No other details are clear. Therefore, we can date
them only to the span of years from 55/4 B.C.E. to 183/4 C.E.

| | | | |
|---|---|---|---|
| M71 1456 | M75 093 | GH78 183 | M72 2306 |
| 21 mm | 23 mm | 19 mm | 22 mm |
| 8.27 g | 7.30 g | 8.23 g | 9.06 g |
| | | | |
| M71 2034 | M75 193 | GH78 068 | M77 1181 |
| 21 mm | 25 mm | 22 mm | 20 mm |
| 5.86 g | 9.29 g | 10.19 g | 5.11 g |
| | | | |
| M72 2213 | M77 066 | M77 110 | |
| 26 mm | 22 mm | 19 mm | |
| 8.75 g | 8.24 g | 7.05 g | |

   The following have only the bust of Melqart visible on the obverse and
therefore must be dated to the span of the preceding plus the time that covers
the next series, that is, to 195/6 C.E.

| | |
|---|---|
| M72 2283 | M72 2305 |
| 23 mm | 23 mm |
| 7.17 g | 5.99 g |

*The Autonomous Period: the Melqart/Temple Series (Ae)*

M75 214          Obv: Laureate bust of Melqart with          195/6 C.E.
27 mm            inscription around worn away.
10.69 g          Rev: Temple of the Koinon of Phoenicia
                 with eight columns. Around, [K]OINO[Y
                 ΦOI]NIKHC. Beneath, AKT (321).

M71 1424         Obv: Same as above, with TYPOYMH-            "
26 mm            TPOΠOΛEWC around.
11.16 g          Rev: Same as above, with KOINOY
(pl. 8)          ΦOINIKHC around. Beneath, AKT
                 (321).

M71 1468         Obv: Same as above.                          "
26 mm            Rev: Same as above, with KOINOY
11.37 g          ΦOINIKHC around and *lṣr* inside at
(pl. 8)          right.

M75 180          Obv: Same as above, with [TY]PO[Y          Late 2nd
25 mm            MHTPO]ΠOΛ[EWC] around.                    century C.E.
8.54 g           Rev: Same as above, with [KOI]NOY

(pl. 9)            ΦΟΙΝΙΚΗC around but no other inscriptional material legible.

The next series of coins are those of the 3rd century C.E. Because they bear
the images of the emperors on the obverse and because they were struck under
the authority and in honor of individual emperors, we shall list them
accordingly. The coins do not bear dates. Therefore, we assign them to the
categories of the dates of the tenures of the individual emperors. All the coins in
this series are of bronze (listed as Ae).

*Coins of Caracalla, (196-)211-17 C.E.*

M74 139         Obv: Laureate bust of Caracalla facing right.
26-27 mm        Rev: A male figure wearing a toga performing a sacrifice
11.72 g         over an altar at left. (This seems to be the coin of Hill 1965:
(pl. 10)        270, no. 370, pictured as pl. 32: 8.) Reading around,
                SEPT[V]R[VSMETPOCOLONI].

KS70 672        Obv: Same as above, with portion of legend reading
25 mm           IMPMAV. . . .
8.07 g          Rev: Same as above, with inscription reading only COL-
                TVR. . . .

M75 215         Obv: Laureate bust of Caracalla facing right. Around,
26 mm           [IMPMAVR]ANTONINVS.
9.40 g          Rev: Agonistic table supporting two prize crowns. (Not
(pl. 9)         visible: palm branch on either side, murex shell beneath.)
                Above, ACTIA; beneath in exergue, [ER]ACL[IA]. Around,
                [SEPTVRVSMETROCOLONI].

M71 1573        Obv: Laureate bust of Caracalla facing right.
24 mm           Rev: A figure standing with both arms down. Behind at
11.00 g         right, Victory on a pedestal extending a wreath. (The figure
(pl. 10)        should be Astarte but the right arm should be lifted. The
                closest to this is Hill 1965: pl. 34: 7.) All other details are worn
                away.

*Coins of Macrinus, 217-18 C.E.*

M71 1451        Obv: Laureate bust of one who appears to be Macrinus with
20 mm           a broad, flat collar. The coin is badly pitted.
7.43 g          Rev: The Phoenician Koinon from quarter perspective.
(pl. 10)        Around, SEPTVRO[METROCOLON]. Beneath, upside
                down, TEMP.

*Coins of Diadumenian, 218 C.E.*

M77 1179        Obv: Youthful bust of Diadumenian facing right with
20 mm           legend around, [MOP]DIA[DV]MENIANVS[CAES].

8.06 g              Rev: Galley with murex shell above. Around, [SEPTVR-
(pl. 11)            VS]METRP. Below, COLON.


## Coins of Elagabalus, 218 C.E.

M75 277            Obv: Youthful laureate bust of Elagabalus facing right with
20 mm              legend around, IMPCAESMAVR [ANTONINVS].
7.45 g             Rev: Temple of the Phoenician Koinon from quarter
(pl. 11)           perspective with murex shell and palm branch beneath.
                   Around, SEPT[VRVS]METRO[COINV] . . . NIC.

M75 245            Same coin as above, but very worn. (All inscriptional
21 mm              material is worn away.)
5.86 g
(pl. 12)

M74 027            Obv: Laureate bust of Elagabalus facing right with legend
28-29 mm           around, CAESMAVANTONINVSAV[G].
18.17 g            Rev: Astarte placing right hand on trophy as she is
(pl. 12)           crowned by Nike from the right. Palm tree in left field;
                   murex shell in right. Around, SEPT IM TVRO. Below,
                   [C]OLO.

M75 244            Same coin as above, but with all inscriptional material
26 mm              worn away except for final . . . VRO on the reverse.
9.99 g
(pl. 11)


## Coins of Elagabalus, 219-22 C.E.

KS71 1417          Obv: Same as above, with IMPMAVAN TONINVSAVG
28 mm              around.
14.25 g            Rev: Same as M74 027 above, but with [TVRIO]RVM
                   around.

GH78 063           Obv: Same as above, with . . . MANTON . . . around and a
28 mm              countermark on the bust that pictures a helmeted head.
14.25 g            Rev: Same as above, with . . . VM around.

M75 027            Same as above but broken, with only . . . MAV AN . . . on
                   the obverse and . . . RI O . . . on the reverse.

M77 1270           Same as above, but worn. A countermark with an emper-
30 mm              or's bust appears in the lower right of the obverse. The
7.86 g             legend on the obverse is worn away. On the reverse we can
(pl. 12)           read . . . O RVM.

M75 211            Same as above, but worn. No inscriptional material
26 mm              legible.
11.38 g

| M71 1574 | Same as above, with . . . CMAVANTO NINVSAVG on |
| 27 mm | the obverse, TVRI O [RVM] on the reverse. |
| 13.90 g | |
| (pl. 13) | |

| GH77 038 | Same as above, but very worn. |
| 27 mm | |
| 10.76 g | |
| (pl. 12) | |

| M72 2297 | Same as above, with [C]AESMAVANT[ONI]NVSAV[G] |
| 27 mm | on the obverse, [TV]RI O RVM on the reverse. |
| 13.87 g | |

| M75 256 | Obv: Laureate bust of Elagabalus facing right, legend worn |
| 21 mm | away. |
| 6.65 g | Rev: Temple facade of six columns with goddess Astarte |
| (pl. 13) | standing beneath the arch. Other details are unclear. |
| | They should include Nike, a palm tree and a murex shell. |
| | The inscription around is worn away. |

| M75 302 | Same as above, but very badly worn. |
| 21 mm | |
| 8.10 g | |

| M71 1450 | Same as above, but corroded and broken. |

| M72 2217 | Same as above, but very badly worn. |
| 25 mm | |
| 8.21 g | |

*Coins of Julia Maesa, 219-22 C.E.*

| GH77 1199 | Obv: Bust of Julia with crescent in her hair, facing right. |
| 27 mm | Rev: Astarte placing right hand on trophy as she is crowned |
| 13.05 g | by Nike from the right. Palm tree in left field, murex shell in |
| (pl. 13) | right. Around, TVRI O RVM. |

*Coins of Gordianus III, 238-44 C.E.*

| M74 097 | Obv: Laureate bust of Gordianus facing right with |
| 29 mm | legend around, IMPGORDIANVS PIVSFELAVG. |
| 17.04 g | Rev: A seminude goddess (Nike?) extending her right |
| (pl. 14) | arm over a palm tree at left, with murex shell at right |
| | and a bird (?) beneath. Between the palm tree and the |
| | goddess, the letter N. Above the murex shell, the letter I. |
| | Around, COL TV R METR. |

*Coins of Phillip II (?), 247-49 C.E.*

| M75 249 | Obv: Bust of one who appears to be Phillip II, with |

22 mm           radiate crown, facing right. The legend around is worn
8.18 g          away.
                Rev: Nike standing with wreath held out in right hand.
                All else is worn away. (This is possibly a coin of Valerian.)

## Coins of Decius Trajan, 249-51 C.E.

M72 2282        Obv: Bust of Decius Traianvs with radiate crown, facing
28 mm           right. Around, . . . T]RAIANVSAVG.
9.58 g          Rev: Nude Diomede standing to left with right foot on rock,
(pl. 14)        left arm resting on spear. A chlamys hangs over his left
                arm. His right hand holds a palladium. Beneath it, in left
                field, is the murex shell. Around, COLTV RO MET.

## Coins of Trebonianus Gallus, 251-53 C.E.

KS71 1310       Obv: Laureate bust of Trebonianus facing right. Because
22 mm           of corrosion the legend around is only partially legible
(pl. 14)        but reads [IMPCG]VIB[IVSTREBO]GALL[VSAVG].
                Rev: Three figures in a galley, the central figure towering
                taller than the others. Around, COLTVR O [MET]. (This
                reverse is not listed in Hill 1965. I hesitate to identify the
                three figures.)

## Coins of Valerian, 253-60 C.E.

M75 221         Obv: Radiate bust of Valerian facing right with legend
27 mm           around, IMPCPLICVALERIANVSAVG.
11.43 g         Rev: Two baetyls with olive tree between, a dolphin and
(pl. 15)        a murex shell below. Around, COLTV[RO MET]RO.
                (This coin is pictured in Babelon 1902: pl. 38: 24.)

M77 1240        Obv: Same as above, but with variance in the legend,
28 mm           which reads IMPLICVALERIANVSAVG.
15.69 g         Rev: Nude Apollo(?) with right hand stretched over
(pl. 15)        an incense altar at the left. Two other tall objects at
                right, one of which may be a palm tree. Around, COL T[VRO
                MET].

M75 436         Obv: Slightly bearded radiate bust facing right with
27 mm           IMPCPL[ICVALERIA]NVSAVG around.
16.64 g         Rev: A river god with a reed in his left hand, his right
(pl. 15)        hand held over an altar with a murex shell above. Around,
                COLTVR OMETR.

KS72 2102       Obv: Same as above, but with illegible inscription.
27 mm           Rev: A river god, clothed in himation, standing with a
(pl. 15)        reed in his left hand. His right hand is held out to an object
                that could be a stone with a plant growing out of it. Around,
                COLTVR O MET.

KS71 1482    Obv: Radiate bust with IMPCPLICVALERIANVSAVG
27 mm        around.
15.87 g      Rev: Seminude Tyche standing with a cruciform standard
             in her right hand. There is a pedestal with a goddess atop
             (Victory?) at the right and a murex shell at Tyche's feet.
             Around, COLTYR[OMET].

There is nothing sensational about this evidence that I have just reviewed. Copper coins are humdrum material. They were humdrum in their own time, for they were the coins of small transactions. Silver or gold coins would have been sensational, for silver and gold seldom last the centuries. Not for lack of durability, of course, but for the fact that they would more likely be found if lost, and if not lost, they would have been claimed for jewelry either as is or melted down for the metal that they were. We found only one gold coin in our six seasons of excavation (it was stolen) and less than a dozen of silver. The bulk of what we found were the coppers that people lost in their daily routines of life, the coppers that were the common currency of common folk. It was the money that people carried about with them that was most easily lost—and in that regard it might be wise to observe that we always find more small coins than large ones. It was the small coins that were most easily lost. When the entire corpus of our finds turns out to be large coins, as for the first half of the 3rd century C.E., it must be that those were the only coins available in copper. And it is a bit ironic that as soon as the Roman government introduced small coppers, they promptly came into dominance. Judging by comparative weight, one suspects, of course, that it took ten small Roman coppers to purchase what one copper tetradrachma purchased a hundred years prior.

With these particular coppers from Tyre, however, we verify what is stated in the excerpt from Josephus' writings, with which I prefaced this composition —that Tyrian money was common currency in the Upper Galilee. It is part of a pattern of factors that are the peculiar features of Upper Galilean economy. Eric M. Meyers has pointed out some of the other features in his discussion of Galilean regionalism that appears in *BASOR* 221: 93-101. It was an area that was tied to the Golan with distinctive features of pottery, an area of architectural conservativism that used local materials for construction, an area of limited goods for export. Linguistically, the Jewish population used Aramaic predominantly and Hebrew considerably. There was much less use of Greek there than in the Galilee district immediately to the south. Meyers has shown that there was a culturo-economic vicinity that comprised Tetracomia within the Upper Galilee, and the numismatic evidence indicates that the Upper Galilee segment, at least, looked to Tyre as the chief center of economic trade and money supply. How much more was included in the geographical periphery of Tyre we can only know as additional coin evidence is found from other sites inland, north and south from the ancient city.[8]

There is inscriptional material on these coins that can be of value to a paleographer interested in the evolution of the Greek scripts. Most observable are the transitions of form in the *omega* and the *sigma* that appear repeatedly in the legends of these coins. Lacking other evidence, the forms in which these letters appear can tell us whether a coin is early or late in a period that spans a half century or more. There are other shifts in the forms of letters that are just as significant, though less obvious. Were it my concern to do a study of Greek paleography, I would make them a point of focus. Less could be said for the few forms of Phoenician letters that appear: the *lamed*, the *ṣade*, the *reš*, and, to lesser degree, the *mem* and the *bet*. It is only because dating is not a central problem in these corpora of coins that I have not dealt with this facet of the material.

Of central interest to me has been what I have called the iconography of the coins. I suspect that the reason for this is the fact that I began this study mostly out of an intrigue with the city of Tyre itself. It struck me as a matter of note that a city so ancient and so thoroughly conquered by Alexander the Great could continue as a place of importance in the world. I fancied that there must be some clues to this in the coins that were struck there, and I now feel that my fancies led to some substantial observations. Most important from an economic point of view is the fact that Tyre continued for a long time as a supplier of money and, concomitantly, as a center of trade in the Levant. Connected to that in an integral way, however, is the spirit and pride of a city that could continue so long against both odds and competition. Certainly the location was not more than part of the key to that, for there were other ports of access to the east in Greco-Roman times that made Tyre only one of several. Its tradition as a port of entry and a producer of certain valued commodities played an even stronger part than its location in producing the tenacity and strength that we are able to observe. The symbols depicted on the coins have given us a rather precise picture of what that tradition comprised. The little murex shell, the city's gods and their accouterments, the galley and other symbols of the sea, and, finally, the rich lore of tales concerning the city's history all combine to give us a strong, clear picture of what helped the merchants of Tyre to play a continued role of importance in the commerce of the Near East.

At Khirbet Shemaᶜ, Meiron, and Gush Ḥalav we have seen which of the coins of Tyre were most commonly in the hands—or in these cases, out of the hands, so to speak—of the people who lived within range of its economic influence. Discounting the silver to a great degree, because it could not as likely survive the hands of men through time, the bronze coins that we unearthed must be the bronze coins that were in greatest supply through the periods represented by our excavations. The other types that are known through chance discoveries here and there must have been in rarer supply. The mundane list of finds that is the core of this chapter is a rather accurate purview, I think, of just which coins were most common. In these excavations of village sites we have been able to open the purses of the peasants who lived there and get an intimate view of this important aspect of their daily lives. A person's purse is not the most important possession of that person's life, to be sure, but it is an essential thing, and because of that, there must be something essential about focusing on such an aspect of life in a time past. These were a people who knew the name of Tyre as the name of the big city nearest them. These were a people who used coins on a daily basis, and judging from the worn to very worn condition of most of the coins we found, they kept their coins in circulation for prodigious lengths of time. At any given time in their own little history they were using coins from various sources: their own precious Hasmonean coins together with coins of the Roman empire and coins of the cities around them that were able and permitted to strike coins. Chief among these sources of money supply for the Jews of Upper Galilee was the proud old city of Tyre.

## NOTES

[1]There are 1960 coppers in this hoard. All are very small and very worn. Only about one-fourth of the total are legible, but the bulk of the coins are obviously of the 5th century, as are the majority of those that are legible. The deposit date of the hoard, judging from the latest specimens, was likely ca. 520 C.E. A report of this hoard is in progress and will be published soon as part of a preliminary report of the Gush Ḥalav excavations, *BASOR* 233.

[2]Evidence from a hoard that was reportedly found at Gush Ḥalav and published by H. Hamburger in 1954 (*Israel Exploration Journal* 4: 201-26) lends considerable corroboration to the evidence we have found. The contents of the hoard are summarized as follows on p. 201: "In 1948 Major H. Ophir acquired in Nazareth a hoard of coins from a villager of Gush Ḥalav (Arab el-Jish, Greek Gischala) in Upper Galilee. The only available information was that the coins were found inside a pottery jar, while the foundations of a house at Gush Ḥalav were being dug. The jar has not been preserved. The finder cleaned the coins superficially as they were covered with a thick brown crust. The present owner attempted a further cleaning with lemon-juice. The silver coins were quickly restored to their old lustre; the bronze coins were later cleaned chemically with the help of the Department of Antiquities, Jerusalem. The hoard consists of 237 coins, viz. (1) 180 Syrian tetradrachms from Nero to Elagabalus, but mainly of the time of Caracalla and Macrinus; (2) 22 Roman denarii from Septimius Severus to Geta; (3) 35 coins of provincial cities, mainly Tyre (!), from Alexander Severus to Philippus." Noting the great number of coins from Tyre relative to other sources, Hamburger studied several private collections in Israel to find that "not a single collection contained a coin which could be ascribed to any of the Palestinian mints" as he sought to determine whether this pattern might be a mere coincidence or due to the fact that more remote towns were called upon to mint coins less frequently (205). One should see a tabulation of all his data to determine whether it covers the entire period for which we found such evidence before taking this as an established rule.

[3]More specifically, at Khirbet Shemaᶜ we found 3 Roman imperial coins plus 5 from Palestine (a total of 8), compared to 4 or more coins from Tyre for the 1st century. At Meiron we found 7 Roman imperial coins plus 15 local Palestinian coins (a total of 22), as compared to 17 from Tyre for that period.

[4]More specifically, at Khirbet Shemaᶜ we found 5 Roman imperial coins, compared to 8 coins from Tyre for the 2nd century. At Meiron, we found 3 Roman imperial plus 5 other local coins for the 2nd century, compared to 35 from Tyre.

[5]There may actually have been a larger supply of Tyrian coins in the Lower Galilee than previously supposed. Meshorer (1976: 54-71) has investigated a hoard found at Migdal in which there were 74 coins of Tyre, 15 of Ace, 17 of Gadara, 14 of Nysa-Scythopolis, 10 of Tiberias, 9 of Hippus, 8 of Diocaesareia, 2 of Gaba, and 1 each of Dium, Abila, and Byblos. This is out of a total of 188 Greek imperial bronzes that range from the times of Titus to Elagabalus.

[6]Excavations at Khirbet Shemaᶜ indicated that the only exportable commodity from that site was olive oil. At nearby Meiron we found a woodworking industry of the 4th century in addition to evidence of the processing of olives. Woodworking may have been done earlier than the 4th century as well. If so, furniture and parts for boats may have been exported to Tyre.

[7]The uniqueness of M77 1041 consists of the spelling, MHTPOΠOΛIC for MHTPOΠOΛEWC, and the two forms of *sigma* that are found in the same inscription. Consult the illustration in pl. 5 to see that the *sigma* at the end of IEPAΣ is a modification of the older form while the *sigma* at the end of MHTPOΠOΛIC is the newer, "C" form. Note M77 1045 to see that some later coins actually retained the older form of the letter, a letter that was in rapid transition at that point in time.

[8]Because of the political unrest in Lebanon I have twice been prevented from visiting the ancient site of Tyre and from resident work at the American University in Beirut. In the meantime, H. J. Katzenstein has undertaken an even more ambitious study than I set out to do. When completed, his work should be definitive.

# PREFACE TO THE PLATES*

The coins I present here to illustrate the text of this little study fall short of what I would like to present. Because I did not take over the task of studying these coins until 1972, I have had less than complete control of the coins of 1970-71. In part, this has meant that I did not acquire excellent photographs of all of them. Normally, the coins are loaned to me by the Israeli Department of Antiquities for a period of one year. After that time they must be returned, and I no longer have access to them. Whatever I photograph in the time I have available to me outside my full-time teaching duties has had to be done during that year. The best of the photographs presented here are the work of Hank van Dijk, Sr., master photographer of the Department of Art at Duke University, who served us in most of our seasons of work. Unfortunately, he was not able to do that service for us in every season, and for those times, the quality of the work has suffered. There were coins I simply cannot illustrate because the photographs I have are not good enough to publish and the coins concerned are no longer accessible to me. For that I can only apologize. What I do present will only illustrate what I have presented in print. To do that in a manner that is clear to the nonspecialist who will read this, I have enlarged most of the illustrations. To get an indication of the size, therefore, one must note the diameter measurements in millimeters that are given with each specimen. For more complete illustrations of known types the reader may consult Hill (1965) and Babelon (1902).

As with the catalog of finds in the fourth chapter, I am here using our own registry numbers for identification. In that system, KS represents Khirbet Shema[c], M represents Meiron, and GH, Gush Halav. The number that immediately follows the letter stands for the season. A number such as M74 044, by way of example, would mean coin no. 44 of the 1974 season at Meiron.

*These plates were prepared for ASOR by Graphic Reproductions of Durham, N.C., whose cooperation is gratefully acknowledged.

PLATE 1

M75-128. The reverse of a coin struck at Tyre in the third century B.C.E. The specimen is corroded but note the war club to the left of the eagle.

KS71-1560, 14mm, 202-187 B.C.E.

Examples of dilepta from the Seleucid period. On the first we see the bust of Antiochus III, with AN[TIOXOY BA] ΣIΛEΩ Σ on the reverse. On the second we see the bust of Antiochus IV, with ANTIO [XOY BAΣIΛEΩΣ] on the reverse. On the third, the bust of Demetrius II and . . . BAΣIΛEΩΣ on the reverse. It is dated H Ξ P, which reads 168 in the Greek numeral system. The fourth specimen is also a coin of Demetrius II with the same date on the reverse. The fifth and sixth specimens are typical of the condition in which we find these coins. In neither case can I identify them beyond saying that they have a Seleucid bust on the obverse and a palm tree on the reverse.

M75-342, 15mm, 175-164 B.C.E.

KS71-1369, 13mm, 144/3 B.C.E.

KS71-1497, 14mm, 144/3 B.C.E.

M74-244, 12mm,

M75-291, 12mm,

## PLATE 2

Enlargements of Seleucid dilepta.

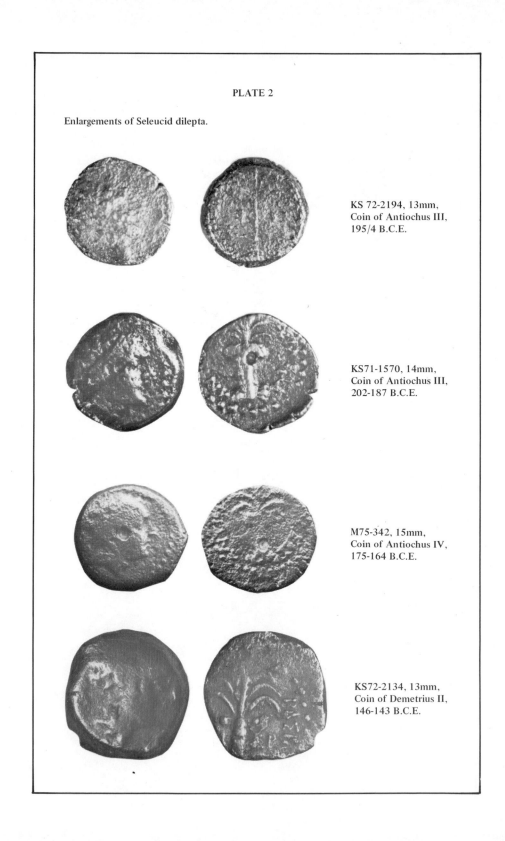

KS 72-2194, 13mm,
Coin of Antiochus III,
195/4 B.C.E.

KS71-1570, 14mm,
Coin of Antiochus III,
202-187 B.C.E.

M75-342, 15mm,
Coin of Antiochus IV,
175-164 B.C.E.

KS72-2134, 13mm,
Coin of Demetrius II,
146-143 B.C.E.

PLATE 3

Coins of the Tyche/war galley series. The first two specimens are from the period 98/7 B.C.E. to 84/85 C.E. On the obverse we see the bust of Tyche. On the reverse, the galley moving left with IEPAΣ inscribed above and 1sr (Phoenician characters) below. The third specimen is from the period 93 - 196 C.E. On its reverse we see the Tyrian monogram plus IEPA[C]/ ΜΗΤΡΟΠ[0]/ΛΕWC.

M74-237, 18mm,
98/7 B.C.E. - 84/5 C.E.

M77-102, 18mm,
98/7 B.C.E. - 84/5 C.E.

M72-2145, 17mm,
93-196 C.E.

PLATE 4

The Tyche/palm trees series. The features common to all are the bust of Tyche on the obverse and the date palm with fruit on the reverse. Details of the reverse differ.

M72-2130, 15mm.
On the reverse we see L plus Phoenician *waw* or *kaph* (6 or 20) and IEP AΣ across the field. 120/19 or 106/5 B.C.E.

M72-2144, 16mm.
On the reverse we read AN (51) and IEP AΣ. 75/4 B.C.E.

KS72-2266, 16mm.
On the reverse we read ΛΣ (230) and, around the Tyrian monogram plus ΜΗΤΡΟΠΟΛ - ΕΩΣΙΕΡΑΣ .

PLATE 5

Tyche/palm tree series (continued).

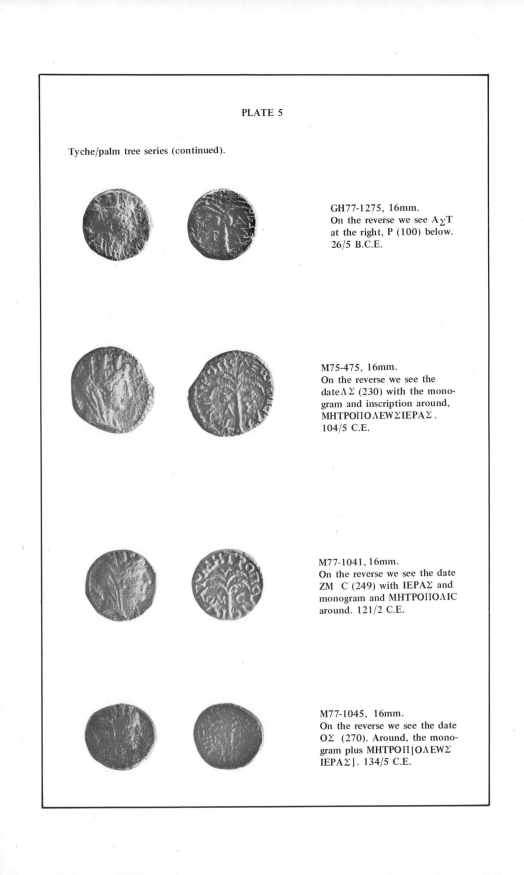

GH77-1275, 16mm.
On the reverse we see AχT
at the right, P (100) below.
26/5 B.C.E.

M75-475, 16mm.
On the reverse we see the
date ΛΣ (230) with the monogram and inscription around,
ΜΗΤΡΟΠΟΛΕΩΣΙΕΡΑΣ.
104/5 C.E.

M77-1041, 16mm.
On the reverse we see the date
ZM C (249) with ΙΕΡΑΣ and
monogram and ΜΗΤΡΟΠΟΛΙC
around. 121/2 C.E.

M77-1045, 16mm.
On the reverse we see the date
ΟΣ (270). Around, the mono-
gram plus ΜΗΤΡΟΠ[ΟΛΕΩΣ
ΙΕΡΑΣ]. 134/5 C.E.

PLATE 6

The Melqart/war club series. On the obverse we see the laureate bust of Melqart facing right. On the reverse, the war club within a wreath and inscription across the face of the coin.

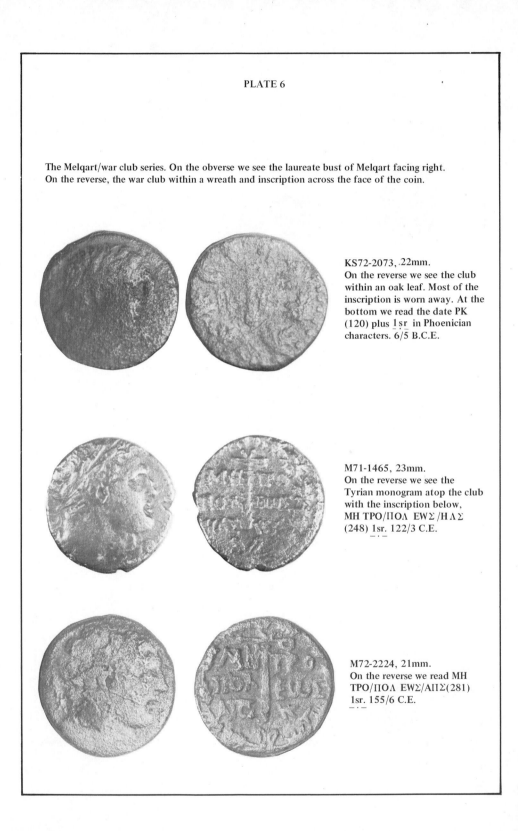

KS72-2073, 22mm.
On the reverse we see the club within an oak leaf. Most of the inscription is worn away. At the bottom we read the date PK (120) plus 1 s r in Phoenician characters. 6/5 B.C.E.

M71-1465, 23mm.
On the reverse we see the Tyrian monogram atop the club with the inscription below, MH TPO/ΠΟΛ ΕΩΣ /ΗΛΣ (248) 1sr. 122/3 C.E.

M72-2224, 21mm.
On the reverse we read MH TPO/ΠΟΛ ΕΩΣ/ΑΠΣ(281) 1sr. 155/6 C.E.

PLATE 7

The Melqart/war club series (continued).

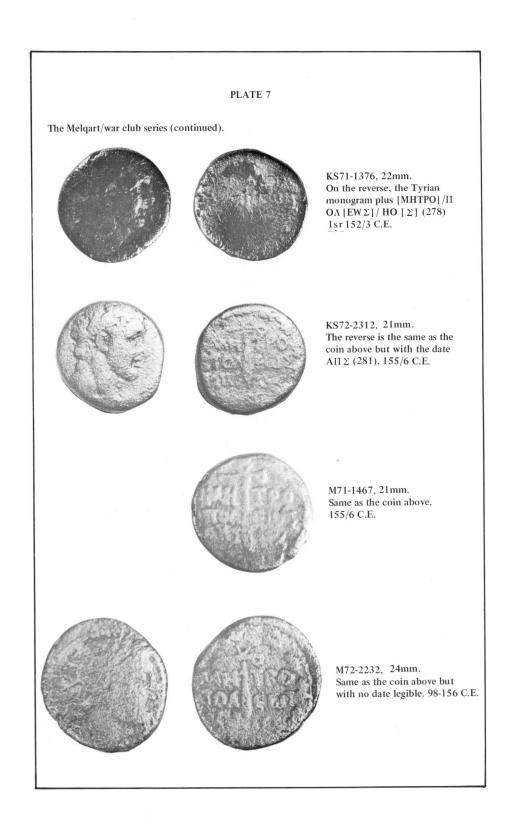

KS71-1376, 22mm.
On the reverse, the Tyrian
monogram plus [MHTPO] /Π
OΛ [EW Σ] / HO [ Σ] (278)
1sr 152/3 C.E.

KS72-2312, 21mm.
The reverse is the same as the
coin above but with the date
AΠ Σ (281). 155/6 C.E.

M71-1467, 21mm.
Same as the coin above.
155/6 C.E.

M72-2232, 24mm.
Same as the coin above but
with no date legible. 98-156 C.E.

PLATE 8

The Melqart/war club series (continued).

M75-181, 21mm.
On the reverse, the inscription
TYPOY/MH T[PO]/ΠΟΛ
EW[C]/HT (308) 1sr. 182/3 C.E.

The Melqart/Koinon series. On the obverse is the laureate bust of Melqart with TYPOYMHT-
POΠOΛEWC around. On the reverse, the temple of the Phoenician Koinon with KOINOY
ΦΟΙΝΙΚΗC around and the date AKT (321) beneath.

M71-1424, 26mm.
As described above. 195/6 C.E.

M71-1468, 26mm.
As above but with 1sr in
Phoenician characters at the
right of the temple facade.
195/6 C.E.

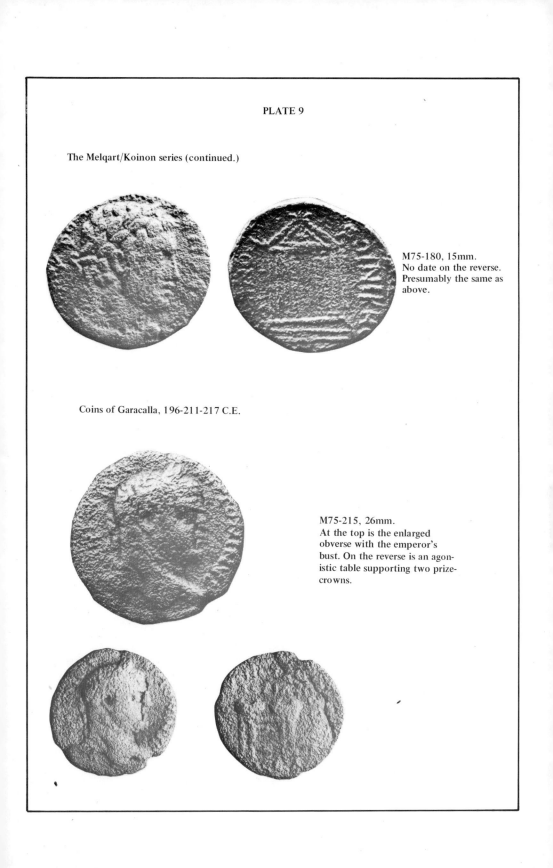

PLATE 9

The Melqart/Koinon series (continued.)

M75-180, 15mm.
No date on the reverse.
Presumably the same as
above.

Coins of Garacalla, 196-211-217 C.E.

M75-215, 26mm.
At the top is the enlarged
obverse with the emperor's
bust. On the reverse is an agonistic table supporting two prize-
crowns.

PLATE 10

Coins of Caracalla (continued).

M74-139, 26-27mm.
On the reverse we see a male
figure in a toga performing a
sacrifice over an altar.

M71-1573, 20mm.
The coin is very worn but on
the reverse we see a figure that
should be Astarte being crowned
by a Victory on the pedestal at
the right.

Coin of Macrinus, 217-218 C.E.

M71-1451, 20mm.
On the obverse is the bust of
the young emperor with a broad,
flat collar. On the reverse, the
Phoenician Koinon from quarter perspective. The inscription
around reads SEPTVRO
[METROCOLON]. Beneath,
written upside down, is TEMP.

PLATE 11

Coin of Diadumenian, 218 C.E.

M77-1179, 20mm. The legend around the youthful bust reads [MOP] DIA [DV] MENIANVS [CAES]. On the reverse is a galley with a murex shell above, [SEPTVREVS] METRP around and COLON below.

Coins of Elagabalus, 218 C.E.

M75-277, 20mm. The legend around the laureate bust reads IMPACAESMAVR [ANTONINVS]. On the reverse is the temple of the Phoenician Koinon from quarter perspective with murex shell and palm branch beneath. The inscription around reads SEPT [VRVS] METRO [COLONI] . . . NIC.

M75-244, 26mm. On the reverse we see Astarte placing her right hand on a trophy as she is crowned by Nike from the right.

PLATE 12

Coins of Elagabalus, 218 C.E. (continued).

M75-245, 21mm.
A worn specimen of the preceding example with the
Phoenician Koinon from quarter
perspective on the reverse.

M74-027, 28-29mm.
The inscription on the obverse
reads CAESMAVANTONINVSAV
[G]. On the reverse is Astarte
placing her hand on a trophy as
she is crowned by Nike. The inscription around reads SEPT
IM TVRO. Below, [C]OLO.

Coins of Elagabalus, 219-222 C.E. The identifying feature of the coins in this group is the
fact that the reverse inscription reads merely TVRIORVM.

M77-1270, 30mm.
A countermark with an emperor's
bust appears in the lower right
of the obverse. On the reverse is
the Astarte scene with [TV] RI
O[RVM] around.

GH77-038, 27mm.
A worn specimen of the same
type of coin.

PLATE 13

Coins of Elagabalus, 219-222 C.E. (continued).

M71-1574, 27mm.
On the obverse, the bust of
the emperor with [IMP]CMA-
VANTO NINVSAVG. On the
reverse, the Astarte scene with
TVRI O [RVM] around.

M75-256, 21mm.
The coin is quite worn but on this reverse we
see a temple facade of six columns with the
goddess Astarte beneath the arch. Other details
are unclear.

Coin of Julia Maesa, 219-222 C.E. As with the coins of Elagabalus from this period, the
inscription on the reverse reads merely TVRIORVM.

GH77-1199, 27mm.
On the obverse is the bust of
Julia with IVLIAMAE SAAVG
around. On the reverse, the
Astarte scene with TV RI O
RVM.

PLATE 14

Coin of Gordianus III, 238-244 C.E.

M74-097, 29mm.
Around the laureate bust of
Gordianus is the legend
IMPGORDIANVS PIVSFELA-
VG. On the reverse is a seminude goddess extending her
arm over a palm tree. The letter
N appears beside the palm. On
the other side of the goddess is
a bird, a murex shell and the
letter I. The inscription around
reads COL TV R METR.

Coin of Decius Trajan, 249-251 C.E.

M72-2282, 28mm.
Decius with radiate crown and
the legend around, . . . T]RAI-
ANVSAVG. On the reverse,
nude Diomede stands with right
foot on a rock, left arm on a
spear. The murex shell is in left
field, COLTV RO MET around.

Coin of Trebonian Gallus, 251-253 C.E.

KS71-1310, 22mm.
The legend on the obverse is
only partly legible. On the
reverse are three figures in a
galley.

PLATE 15

Coins of Valerian, 253-260 C.E. The busts are regularly with radiate crown. The legend on the obverses reads IMP(CP)LICVALERIANVSAVG.

M75-221, 27mm.
On the reverse are the two rocks with an olive tree between, a dolphin and murex shell below. The inscription around reads COLTV[RO MET]RO.

M77-1240, 28mm.
On the reverse is nude Apollo with right hand stretched over an incense altar. The two objects at the right are unclear. One may be a palm tree. Only the first part of the inscription around is legible.

M75-436, 27mm.
On the reverse is a river god with a reed in his left hand and his right hand held over an altar with a murex shell above. The inscription around reads COLTVR OMETR.

KS72-2102, 27mm.
The reverse of this coin bears the same motif as the one above but with some variation in the object that appears to be an altar

PLATE 16

Coin of Valerian, 253-260 C.E.  (continued).

KS71-1482,  27 mm.
The full legend is visible on the
obverse.  On the reverse is seminude Tyche with a cruciform
standard in her right hand.  There
is a pedestal with a goddess atop
at the right and a murex shell
at Tyche's feet.
Around is COLTYR  [OMET]

Late additions from the 1978 season.

GH78-073,  21 mm.
Ar. didrachm of Antiochus II (?)
with Hellenic bust on the obverse
and an eagle on the reverse.  At
the left of the eagle is the Tyrian
club with A/RE above.  Over the
right shoulder is the palm branch
and beneath it, A  and the
date, I ("13") which may signify
189/8 B.C.E.
Around is ANTIOXOY.

GH78-063,  26 mm.
Coin of Elagabalus
enlarged so as to better
see the countermark on
the bust which seems
to be a helmeted head.

# BIBLIOGRAPHY

Babelon, E.
   1902 *Traité des monnaies grecques et romaines*, vol. 2. Paris: Bibliotheque Nationale.
Baramki, D.
   1961 *Phoenicia and the Phoenicians.* Beirut: American University of Beirut.
   1968 *The Coins Exhibited in the Archaeological Museum of Beirut.* Beirut: American University of Beirut.
Boyle, I., ed.
   1955 *The Ecclesiastical History of Eusebius Pamphilus.* Trans. C. F. Cruse. Grand Rapids: Baker Book House.
British Museum
   1899 *Catalogue of the Greek Coins of Galatia, Cappadocia, and Syria.* London: British Museum.
Chami, J. M.
   1967 *De la phénicie.* Beirut: Librairie du Liban.
Fedden, R.
   1965 *The Phoenix Land: the Civilization of Syria and Lebanon.* New York: George Braziller.
Fleming, W. B.
   1915 *The History of Tyre.* Columbia Oriental Studies 10. New York: Columbia University. (Reprinted by AMS Press in 1966.)
Gardner, P.
   1963 *A Catalogue of the Greek Coins in the British Museum: the Seleucid Kings of Syria.* Bologna: Arnaldo Forni.
Gibbon, E.
   1936 *The Decline and Fall of the Roman Empire.* New York: Washington Square Press. (Originally published in 1777.)
Grant, M.
   1968 *Roman History from Coins.* Cambridge: Cambridge University.
   1968 *The Climax of Rome: the Final Achievements of the Ancient World.* Boston: Little, Brown.
   1969 *The Ancient Mediterranean.* New York: Scribner.
Grierson, P.
   1975 *Numismatics.* Oxford: Oxford University.
Halsberghe, G. H.
   1972 *The Cult of Sol Invictus.* Leiden: E. J. Brill.
Hamburger, H.
   1954 A Hoard of Syrian Tetradrachms and Tyrian Bronze Coins from Gush Halav. *Israel Exploration Journal* 4: 201-26.
Harden, D.
   1962 *The Phoenicians. Ancient Peoples and Places.* London: Thames and Hudson.
Herm, G.
   1975 *The Phoenicians: the Purple Empire of the Ancient World.* Trans. C. Hillier. New York: Morrow.
Hill, G. F.
   1965 *A Catalogue of the Greek Coins in the British Museum: Greek Coins of Phoenicia.* Bologna: Arnaldo Forni.
Jacoby, F.

1923 *Die Fragmente der griechischen Historiker.* Berlin: Weidman.

Jidejian, N.

1969 *Tyre Through the Ages.* Beirut: University of Beirut.

Jones, A. N. M.

1964 *The Later Roman Empire.* Oxford: Blackwell.

Jones, H. L., ed. and trans.

1954-60 *The Geography of Strabo,* vols. 2, 7, 8. Cambridge, MA: Harvard University.

Kapelrud, A. S.

    1962a Sidon. Pp. 343-45 in vol. 4 of *Interpreter's Dictionary of the Bible,* ed. G. A. Buttrick, et al. New York/Nashville: Abingdon.

    1962b Tyre. Pp. 721-23 in vol. 4 of *Interpreter's Dictionary of the Bible,* ed. G. A. Buttrick, et al. New York/Nashville: Abingdon.

Katzenstein, H. J.

    1973 *The History of Tyre: from the 2nd Millennium to 538 B.C.* Jerusalem: Shocken Institute for Jewish Research of the Jewish Theological Seminary of America.

Liddell, H. G., and Scott, R.

    1940 *A Greek-English Lexicon.* 9th edition. Oxford: Clarendon Press.

Meshorer, Y.

    1967 *Jewish Coins of the Second Temple Period.* Trans. I. H. Levine. Tel Aviv: Am Hasefer.

    1976 A Hoard of Coins from Migdal. *ᶜAtiqot* 2: 54-71.

Moscati, S.

    1968 *The World of the Phoenicians.* Trans. Weidenfeld and Nicolson, Ltd. New York: Praeger.

Newell, E. T.

    1921 *The First Seleucid Coinage of Tyre.* Numismatic Notes and Monographs 10. New York: American Numismatic Society.

    1923 *Tyrus Rediviva.* New York: American Numismatic Society.

    1936 *The Seleucid Coinages of Tyre.* Numismatic Notes and Monographs 36. New York: American Numismatic Society.

Peckham, J. B., S. J.

    1968 *The Development of the Late Phoenician Scripts.* Cambridge, MA: Harvard University.

Pliny the Elder

    *Natural History,* vols. 3, 6, 8. Trans. Rockham and Jones. Cambridge, MA: Harvard University, 1951-56.

Poedebard, A.

    1939 *Un grand port disparu: Tyr.* Paris: Librairie Orientaliste Paul Geuthner.

Pritchard, J. B.

    1955 *Ancient Near Eastern Texts Relating to the Old Testament.* Princeton: Princeton University Press.

Reece, R.

    1970 *Roman Coins.* London: Ernest Benn, Ltd.

Rogers, E.

    1927 *The Second and Third Seleucid Coinages of Tyre.* Numismatic Notes and Monographs 34. New York: American Numismatic Society.

Rouvier, J.

    1900 *Numismatique des villes de la phénicie.* Beirut: University of Beirut.

Seyrig, H.

    1917 Le cult du soleil en Syrie a l'epoque romain. *Syria* 48: 338-73.

Sperber, D.

1965-70 Costs of Living in Roman Palestine. *Journal of the Social and Economic History of the Orient* 8.3, 9.3, 11.3, 13.1.

    1974   *Roman Palestine, 200-400, Money and Prices*. Ramat-Gan: Bar-Ilan University.

Sutherland, C. H. V.

    1974   *Roman Coins*. London: Barrie and Jenkins, Ltd.

Ward, W. A.

    1968   The Role of the Phoenicians in the Interaction of Mediterranean Civilizations. *Papers Presented to the Archeological Symposium at the American University of Beirut*, ed. W. A. Ward. Beirut: American University of Beirut.

Waterman, L., et al.

    1931   *Preliminary Report of the University of Michigan Excavations at Sepphoris, Palestine, in 1931*. Ann Arbor: University of Michigan.

Whiston, W., ed.

    1902   *The Complete Works of Flavius Josephus*. Chicago: Thompson and Thomas.

Will, E.

    1973   Sur quelques monnaies de Tyre. *Revue numismatique* 15: 80-84.